Race on Campus

Race on Campus

Debunking Myths with Data

Julie J. Park

HARVARD EDUCATION PRESS
CAMBRIDGE, MASSACHUSETTS

Paperback ISBN 978-1-68253-232-4
Library Edition ISBN 978-1-68253-233-1

Library of Congress Cataloging-in-Publication Data
CIP data is on file with the Library of Congress.

Published by Harvard Education Press,
an imprint of the Harvard Education Publishing Group

Harvard Education Press
8 Story Street
Cambridge, MA 02138

Cover Design: Ciano Design
Cover Image: Tom Hoover/Moment/Getty Images
The typefaces used in this book are Joanna Nova and Joanna Sans Nova

For Daniel,
with love from your
favorite Harvard reject

Contents

Introduction

COLLEGES ARE RADICALLY different places than they were just a few decades ago. With growing enrollments of students of color and women, the typical college student is no longer a White male aged eighteen to twenty-two. Universities have also changed how they serve diverse student bodies. At many campuses, chief diversity officers, ethnic studies programs, and multicultural student services offices collaborate to offer students opportunities to learn about issues related to race, class, sexual orientation, religion, and other identities.

For all the strides universities have made in diversifying, a common lament is that they have actually achieved very little. Comments such as "Students just stick to themselves," "People stay in their comfort zones," and, famously, "Why do all the Black kids sit together in the cafeteria?" characterize public perceptions that colleges and universities are starkly and pervasively divided by race. The term *self-segregation* has come to simplistically describe the notion that students of color (a broad term referring to African American, Latinx, Asian American, Pacific Islander, Native American and other Indigenous populations) are insular, retreating to their own racial/ethnic groups instead of mixing with the rest of campus. In a *Georgetown Voice* article entitled "Diversity Beyond the Statistics: Self-Segregation Among Student Groups," a student bemoaned that "the popularity of student cultural associations and the establishment of cultural housing has been counterproductive to the values Georgetown wants to instill through diversity. While I respect and admire the work of these clubs, often the diversity they advance also fosters an environment in which each ethnic group remains with its own."[1]

This writer's thoughts reflect a broader conversation in the public discourse around the question, *Is diversity counterproductive?* It's a legitimate question. After all, what's the point of bringing different types of students to campus if they're just going to stick with themselves?

While on the subject, Is affirmative action still needed? With the Supreme Court ruling in *Fisher II v. Texas*, race-conscious admissions is (likely) here to stay, yet the public remains confused about what affirmative action really is and how it affects students. Many people think that it only helps rich minorities (like say, President Obama's daughter Malia), leaving poorer minorities in the dust. There are thousands of strong students from low-income backgrounds who are disadvantaged in the admissions process, so wouldn't it be better to base any preferences in the admissions system on class instead of race? And what about Asian Americans? Do they really need a SAT score that is 140 points higher than White students or 200 points higher than Black students to get into a top college? It all seems pervasively unfair.

All these questions can make the public wonder if diversity hurts more than it helps, precisely at a time when our country is grappling with serious concerns about our ability to support a diverse democracy. As someone who studies higher education, I hear questions like that all the time. What concerns me, however, is my sense that they are based more on opinion, projections, and anecdotes than on facts and data.

In *Race on Campus: Debunking Myths with Data* I have two big goals. First, I want to challenge pervasive myths on how race works in higher education, both in admissions and campus life, by drawing on the latest empirical research. I draw on statistical analyses that colleagues and I have conducted of large-scale, national, longitudinal datasets—thousands of students attending hundreds of colleges—where we control for key background and experiential characteristics, allowing us to get closer to understanding what factors are potentially influencing an outcome. In other examples I draw on research studies conducted by peers in the field. In all cases, the studies I cite have gone through the rigorous evaluation of publication in peer-reviewed journals, many of which are the top in their respective fields.

I will walk readers through key enduring myths surrounding race, higher education, and the college admissions process. Besides challenging allegations of rampant self-segregation, these myths include the following notions: class-based affirmative action is the true answer to inequality; Asian Americans are harmed by affirmative action; the SAT is a reliable way to measure excellence; and students of color are "mismatched" when they attend selective institutions. With all these perceptions, we need to draw on research and evidence to inform public opinion and policy.

In combining research on admissions with studies on the racial dynamics of campus life, I hope to highlight how the two are really inseparable. Sure, we may talk about them independently in policy discussions, but the issues that affect who comes to campus, and under what conditions, are closely linked to the types of experiences students have once they are enrolled. Simply put, the inequality that stratifies students' pathways to college does not end once classes start. Additionally, some of the stereotypes that fester in discussions about who is qualified to attend what types of institutions carry over to the campus environment, affecting the ways that classmates, faculty, administration, and staff view and treat students of color (we'll see this most glaringly in the debate on mismatch).

As a teaser, I will tell you that the research shows us that far from being insular, students of color are constantly interacting across race in the collegiate setting. Part of this dynamic is that they have little choice at institutions where they are a numerical minority: they constantly interact across race in classrooms, residence halls, intramural sports, and the like. Not only that, they have high levels of close interracial friendship—notably higher than the rate for White students.[2] Counterintuitively, participation in ethnic student organizations, the very clubs that seem like havens for self-segregation, is actually linked with *higher* rates of interacting across race during college.[3] "Recharging" with same-race peers gives students of color the energy they need to mix with the broader campus. Indeed, the data reveal that students' experiences are much more multifaceted than the hour or two they might spend hanging out in the cafeteria with same-race peers. And there's good reason why this recharging time is critically important to their very survival on racially mixed or predominantly White campuses.

Alright, challenging myths with data—got it. The second goal of *Race on Campus* is to unpack the origins of race-related myths in higher education and critique the persistent spread of misinformation. I address the misconceptions and stereotypes behind these myths (e.g., why people get fixated on the example of Malia Obama as a supposed affirmative action beneficiary) by introducing critical research on cognitive biases. An example of this is what pioneering psychologists Amos Tversky and Daniel Kahneman dub the "availability heuristic."[4] Cognitively processing life takes a lot of effort; the brain has to rely on mental shortcuts to process information. In particular, brains rely on information that is easiest or simplest to recall. Sometimes it's the information most recently heard ("I just read in the news that . . . ") or something that resonates with personal experience. Other times it's something that we keep hearing about over and over again. On top of that, it is harder for brains to summon instantly all the possible exceptions—the "but what about" thought. It is much easier to rely on default ways of understanding than it is to entertain a more nuanced understanding of a problem. To be sure, life's challenges and stresses demand that we function on autopilot for many mundane tasks or jobs, and the availability heuristic refers to our tendency to summon examples that we can readily remember and easily recall. While this strategy is certainly helpful for managing day-to-day life, sometimes it can lead us to turn to anecdotes or compelling examples instead of combing through the data and looking for disconfirming evidence.

You may be familiar with Tversky and Kahneman from Kahneman's masterful synthesis of their research, *Thinking Fast and Slow* (it's a really thick book with a pencil on the cover).[5] In it he explains two systems of thought. System 1 is quick and intuitive, relying on mental shortcuts to help the brain come to quick conclusions. Gut feelings? They come from System 1. In contrast, System 2 is slower, more rational and deliberative. Thinking it through, looking at the data, being aware of your own preconceptions and challenging them—that's System 2. Reading through *Thinking Fast and Slow*—or any book highlighting the extent to which we rely on System 1, sometimes to our own detriment (the title of Dan Ariely's *Predictably Irrational* sums up our capacity for judgment)—is illuminating. Most of us see ourselves as logical folks, but the same intuition that makes it possible to navigate modern life means that our brains are susceptible to assumptions and judgments that don't capture the full extent of what's going on. We need both systems to live life, but we also need to keep ourselves in check, knowing very well that some of the smartest folks in the room, like Kahneman and friends, are the first to acknowledge that we're deeply limited creatures.

The tendency to rely on mental shortcuts in processing information (System 1) is doing the public a deep disservice when we assess the state of race relations on college campuses. It's too easy for people to feel confident in their understandings of what is happening on college campuses today, especially for people who attended college at some point. Assessments of campus life get repeated and repeated again, cementing themselves as facts in the public consciousness, per the availability heuristic and other cognitive biases. While personal experience and observation are important, the public needs to look beyond "a single story" to understand the bigger picture that data show.[6]

By helping readers understand why certain race-related myths are so pervasive, *Race on Campus* will help readers examine their assumptions and gain a more informed perspective on diversity in higher education.

Colleges and universities have made tremendous strides in diversifying and supporting diverse student bodies, but we owe it to the next generation of students to use research and data to guide policies and programs, not hunches and assumptions.

AN OVERVIEW

Who should read this book? Everyone! If you're a graduate student, academic, policy maker, educator, everyday citizen—come on in. One of my key goals is to highlight empirical studies on race in a way that is more accessible than the original peer-reviewed journal articles, which are primarily read by academics. Don't get me wrong, academic journals are riveting reading, but it can be tedious to comb through study after study, so I've done that work for you. I've also done my best to write this book in a conversational tone to make it accessible to a wide range of readers. So if you like this book, don't hesitate to pick up more copies for Mother's Day, Teacher Appreciation Week, Boxing Day—you get the picture. I owe tribute to books that have done a great job of bringing social science research to a broader audience, from the original *Why Are All the Black Kids Sitting Together in the Cafeteria?* to *Freakonomics.*

Here's an overview of what *Race on Campus: Debunking Myths with Data* addresses.

Chapter 1:

Black Students and the Cafeteria—What's the Big Fuss?

Who's eating where in the cafeteria, and why do we care so much? This chapter talks about the campus cafeteria as a (mistaken) symbol of all that's wrong with race on college campuses and debunks the myth that students of color pervasively self-segregate during their college years. In fact, numerous studies show that students of color interact more across race and have more close interracial friendships than White students do. I also draw on research to show how organizations that seem like they cultivate self-segregation and deter racial diversity, such as ethnic student organizations, actually foster diverse interactions and significant engagement for students. I use the concept of the availability heuristic to help readers understand why students of color *seem* to be self-segregating when, in reality, their experiences are more diverse and multifaceted.

Chapter 2:
Who's Really Self-Segregating? Sororities, Fraternities, and Religious Groups

On the flip side, organizations like fraternities and sororities are linked to limited engagement with diversity for White students, and affluent White students tend to have friendship groups that are the most homogeneous. I discuss why this is so and why it's easy for us to overlook this, as compared to the critical attention (and blame) focused on students of color. I also look at religious student organizations, another community that is largely divided by race, and explain why this dynamic is less problematic than Greek life on many campuses.

Chapter 3:
Is Class-Based Affirmative Action the Answer?

One of the biggest questions in higher education asks, Is class-based affirmative action the answer to our problems? Some have argued for class-based affirmative action over race-conscious admissions (the current system at most selective institutions), portraying it as an either-or, mutually exclusive decision between considering class (and class alone) versus considering race in combination with numerous factors, including class.[7] I show that institutions need a variety of methods to attract diverse student bodies, including approaches that are both race and class conscious, and also demonstrate the need for institutions to have the *option* to consider race, even in the twenty-first century. I highlight the limitations of anchoring (a type of cognitive fallacy) to challenge the myth that affirmative action is benefiting the "rich Black student" (e.g., Malia Obama) instead of a broader range of students who need an admissions system that considers race.

Chapter 4:

Why Affirmative Action Is Good for Asian Americans

In 2014 the anti–affirmative action movement filed a lawsuit against Harvard University, presenting a group of Asian American students with stellar test scores, outstanding grades, and strong extracurricular activities as the plaintiffs. I debunk the myth that Asian Americans are systematically discriminated against in selective college admissions and show how they benefit from the racially diverse student bodies that affirmative action can produce. I address how Thomas Espenshade and Alexandria Walton Radford's research on test scores linked with the probability of admission has been misunderstood and misrepresented and, thus, has contributed to the exploitation of the Asian American community by the anti–affirmative action movement.

Chapter 5:

Why the SAT and SAT Prep Fall Short

Despite the slight uptick in schools deciding to go SAT-optional, the SAT remains a dominant and hegemonic force in college admissions. The equity of the SAT is threatened by the pervasive inequality that permeates K–12 education, and students have deeply divergent opportunities to master the test. Many critics have focused on the disparities in access to test preparation services. Test prep agencies such as Kaplan and the Princeton Review—which charge hundreds, if not thousands, of dollars—boast that they increase students' scores by hundreds of points. I present research that should further raise eyebrows about the equity of the SAT. Not only do inequities exist in access to test prep services, but, counterintuitively, research suggests that overall gains associated with test prep are minimal and that not all students gain equally from test prep, even when they get the opportunity to take it. Troublingly, these inequities are linked to race.[8]

Overall, the differential benefits students experience from test prep adds to the evidence on how the SAT falls short as an "objective" and "reliable" measure.

Chapter 6:
The Problem of the "Problem of Mismatch"

Before his passing, Justice Antonin Scalia famously remarked about the possibility that African American students can excel at "a less-advanced school, a slower-track school where they do well." The so-called theory of mismatch—the idea that Black, Latinx, and Native American students are out of their league attending highly selective institutions and would do better at "slower-track" institutions—has been hotly debated in the media, as well as in pop social science books such as *David and Goliath*, by Malcolm Gladwell, and *Mismatch*, by Richard Sander and Stuart Taylor.[9] While Scalia's comments reflect gross stereotypes, Sander and Taylor claim to draw on empirical analysis to suggest that attending the most selective schools works against the interests of students of color.[10] Are they right? I engage with Sander and Taylor's work and detail the extensive body of research that refutes mismatch. Troublingly, the discourse on mismatch ignores the assets and savvy that students of color use to succeed in selective institutions of higher education. I also question why mismatch is rarely raised as a concern for the scores of White and Asian American college students who struggle in higher education.

HOW THEN SHOULD WE THINK? A CONCLUSION

In the concluding discussion I provide recommendations for how we can think better about race in higher education, given the pervasiveness of cognitive fallacies. With greater media attention allocated toward boosting socioeconomic diversity on college campuses, it is tempting to assume that universities have achieved their goals when it comes to racial diversity. However, the work of diversity—racial and otherwise—is far from done. I explain how the trend toward prioritizing inclusion is important but falls short without continued attention to diversity and equity and how any emphasis on diversity needs to take place within a broader commitment to addressing inequality and racism, both past and present. Rather than thinking of diversity as a place or status that we can reach and then be done, I explain how the work of diversity and antiracism is never finished and how recognizing the lack of an endpoint can help us engage with the issues more honestly, authentically, and effectively.

* * *

Diversity. It's something people increasingly recognize that we need, but we seem to be at odds over how to foster and support. It's one of our country's greatest strengths, but it's also a source of divisiveness and confusion. I grew up beating a drum for racial diversity and equity early. Growing up Korean American in a predominantly White suburb in Ohio always made me wonder, "Is there something more?" As a campus activist in Nashville during my college days, I got involved in efforts to recruit more students of color to our predominantly White campus. Eventually I realized I could study these things for a living, which led me to my career as an academic.

Part of my interest in writing this book is to share some of my own journey of realizing that I, an academic "diversity expert," have at times missed key pieces of data or jumped to conclusions on issues only to have my preconceptions overturned. Like everyone else on the planet, my System 1 is quite strong, and, really, I'm quite fond of it. At the same time, I know that my worldview and perspective are limited—I am an "n of 1"—and I've been proven wrong many times. However, there's something strangely satisfying about challenging your assumptions—if you're brave enough to try it and are willing to be surprised. I hope you'll join me for the ride.

CHAPTER ONE

Black Students and the Cafeteria—What's the Big Fuss?

ALTHOUGH NOT A COLLEGE CAMPUS, an early scene in the 2004 movie *Mean Girls* sums it up well. On entering her high school cafeteria for the first time, the heroine of the story quickly identifies the complex social arrangements reflected in the tables of students, noting the ones that fall along racial lines. She assesses the scene: "You got your Freshmen, ROTC Guys, Preps, JV Jocks, Asian Nerds, Cool Asians, Varsity Jocks, Unfriendly Black Hotties, Girls Who Eat Their Feelings, Girls Who Don't Eat Anything, Desperate Wannabes, Burnouts, Sexually Active Band Geeks, The Greatest People You Will Ever Meet, and The Worst. Beware of The Plastics."[1] Stereotypes and all, you have to appreciate her ability to distinguish between the tables of nerdy Asians and cool Asians.

When people hear that I study racial diversity on college campuses for a living, the reactions are generally a mix of surprise ("You get paid to do that?") and then lament, which is usually something about how colleges are diverse but what good is it if "students don't mix." If you visit a college dining hall at 12:00 p.m. on any given weekday, it's easy to assume that mixing across race is rare behavior. There are tables and tables of students, but the ones that stick out are those that are filled with students seemingly of the same race or ethnicity eating, laughing, and studying together. In the entire college setting, the college cafeteria is probably the most colloquially cited example of how students "stick to themselves" or "don't really interact much with each other."

There's even a book written about it. I still remember the first time I heard about *Why Are All the Black Kids Sitting Together in the Cafeteria?* by Beverly Daniel Tatum.[2] I was attending a summer program in high school and walking with two (Black) friends who burst into laughter in instant recognition of Tatum's clever title. I laughed along, a little confused since there were so few Black kids to begin with back home in my suburban Ohio cafeteria. But once I got to college, I understood much better. And once I got plugged into the Asian American student community at Vanderbilt, it was easy for me to take my tray upstairs to see if anyone I knew was in the usual spot where people hung out. Downstairs, clusters of other racial/ethnic groups occupied the usual spots, as well as athletes, artsy sorts, and the like.

The racially divided cafeteria evokes a powerful image in our collective consciousness and is also an easy target for those bemoaning the lack of "real" engagement across racial/ethnic lines. A term I often hear is *self-segregation*, as in "students are so self-segregated," or "they choose to self-segregate," as if the system of segregation is one that any group of students would willingly hoist on themselves. Still, the term is casually thrown around, as evidenced by a quick Google search of campus newspapers and media outlets: "Stanford's Silent Segregation," "UF Promoting Racism with New Self-Segregated Housing," and "What to Do About Self-Segregation on Campus?"[3] It's also the subject of many an earnest collegiate town hall meeting. I have memories of sitting in such meetings at multiple campuses and hearing students propose things like a Sit Outside Your Comfort Zone Day, when people are encouraged to sit with someone who they do not ordinarily sit with, as if one day of sitting somewhere else in the dining hall is going to fix the world's racial conflicts. As silly as these proposals feel, they speak to the significance of the cafeteria as a symbol to many of racial balkanization on campus, as well as to the simplistic idea that changing the cafeteria is the key to racial harmony.

The problem with relying on the cafeteria as a primary means of understanding the state of race relations is that it is generally just one (or two, counting dinner) hours of a day that the last time I checked has a full twenty-four hours. What we see in the cafeteria may fall along racial/ethnic lines, but it's also just a slice of students' days. What people often forget are the other hours of the day, the times when students mix across racial/ethnic lines in other spheres of campus life: attending classes that are racially diverse, living in residence halls, engaging in service learning, working in part-time jobs, attacking problem sets in study groups, and getting involved in campus organizations. They may not all be best friends, but something is undeniably going on there.

A consistent finding from studies of interracial contact and friendship is that students of color have markedly *higher* rates of cross-racial engagement than their White peers.[4] Even when controlling for factors such as students' race/ethnicity, actual interest in diversity issues, gender, socioeconomic status, and other key factors, statistical analyses of thousands and thousands of students tell us that students of color are mixing across races at a rate that outpaces their White counterparts. Even when you use methods like asking students to name their friends one at a time and *then* to list their friends' races/ethnicities, which avoids the issue of being primed to think about race when recalling key relationships (e.g., "How many African American friends do you have?"), White students are significantly less likely to have close friends of other races. In a study I did utilizing this method, I found that more than half (51.5 percent) of White students had no close friends of other races. In contrast, only 25.7 percent of African American, 7.7 percent of Latinx, and 15.8 percent of Asian American students had close friendship groups that were racially homogeneous.[5]

Going back to my own cafeteria experience—I still can visualize it well, but there were still plenty of times when we mixed across racial/ethnic lines. I got involved in coalitions with other student of color organizations, some of which I felt more at home in than I did in the Asian American community. Vanderbilt shoved a lot of student groups into a single office, so we became friends and interacted all the time, volunteering for each other's events and cheering one another on. I ended up living in a residence hall with a lot of those artsy-looking folks (and their philosophy-loving compatriots), and they were pretty nice people. The student athletes tended to pop up in my sociology classes. So which was the real Vanderbilt—the racially divided cafeteria at lunchtime or the full twenty-four hours of the day, which usually included a decent amount of time with my closest friends (mostly Asian American), as well as plenty of time mixing across racial/ethnic boundaries? The truth is it was probably somewhere in the middle, but that had more to do with some of the dynamics of that particular campus than anything else.

Why is the cafeteria such a powerful image? Turning to the tools of cognitive science, we can think about the availability heuristic from Tversky and Kahneman, which describes how we revert to the information that can be most easily recalled, or what's "available" in our minds.[6] Not only that, but we use this tendency as a mental shortcut to assess the relative importance of information. If we can remember it, we believe that it's something worth remembering and therefore important and relevant. For many of us, the cafeteria is an image that sticks out, perhaps because it's a space where a wide spectrum of people are thrown together, and yet we can see where people are congregating by race/ethnicity. Or at least we *think* we see it; indeed, we may be seeing only part of the picture. When people comment on the cafeteria, it's usually the question of why Black folks, or Asian folks or whoever, are all sitting together, when there are probably just as many all-White or mostly White tables, depending on the demographics of the institution. I mean, when I taught at Miami University in Ohio, which at the time was well over 80 percent White, mystified people *still* asked why Black students sat together, even though the campus was full of White students clustering together at cafeteria tables, in sororities or fraternities, and in other spaces.

We are used to thinking of White folks as the norm, so much so that we (especially those in the majority) are conditioned to not notice clusters of White people or White people gathering together as unusual. In contrast, people of color, and especially groups of people of color, stick out—to the point where they're often perceived as threatening. An example of this in the news is when a group of Black women was kicked off a tour of Northern California's Napa Valley because they were laughing.[7] Yes, laughing. Their laughter was somehow seen as threatening and disruptive because—well, I really have no idea why. For whatever reason, "Driving While Black" or "Flying While Brown" or "Laughing While Black and Female" are real things. So sometimes the very action of "Existing as a Minoritized Person/People" is deemed exceptional and therefore memorable and worthy of attention. Another example that comes to mind from religious circles is when White people ask me why I go to a predominantly Asian American church. When I flip the question back and ask why so many White people go to church together, let's just say that awkwardness often ensues.

So back to the cafeteria—in short, because Whites are seen as the norm, tables of students of color pop out glaringly, while Whites tend to fade into the background.[8] Tables of students of color becomes a dominant image that seems definitive of student experiences instead of being just a slice of a student's day. It becomes easily recallable information that we associate as the state of campus race relations. Availability heuristic—voila.

THINKING CRITICALLY ABOUT HOW WE SIT TOGETHER

Something critical to consider is that interracial contact and friendship do not happen at random. First, the demography of the campus matters quite a bit. Research studies show that the more racially diverse the student body is, the higher the likelihood of interracial interaction and friendship.[9] Americans generally have a high value for individualism and we think, "Darn it! I can be friends with whomever I want!" We view friendship as a matter of personal preference, not as being shaped by broader social forces. Rarely do we think about how the demography of environments and institutions facilitate or constrain these opportunities.[10] Take the classic admissions brochure photo featuring smiling students of different races. It's a lovely image, but one that is statistically unlikely on many college campuses. If you have a student body of fifteen thousand and a Black enrollment of 3 percent, and you randomly select five students at a time for your photo, 86 percent of the time your photo ends up with zero Black students in it.[11] Your probability of selecting a Black student goes up if you have more Black students in your student body, but this example highlights how these smiling moments that everyone wants—diverse admissions photos and racially mixed cafeteria tables—are deeply shaped by who's actually enrolled in college, which in turn is shaped by patterns of inequality.

Additionally, students are shaped by the subcultures of the university in which they spend the most time. Once again, demography matters, and it has the potential to influence behavior. So certain environments, such as fraternities and sororities dominated by a particular racial/ethnic group (White students), are linked with significantly lower rates of close interracial friendship and, in some studies, lower interracial contact.[12] These types of groups can function as bubbles that shield their members from engaging with the broader diversity of the campus. What is even more worrisome is that this isolation can potentially damage students' attitudes. For example, after being involved in fraternities and sororities for a few years, White students were less likely to support interracial marriage and had higher levels of symbolic racism.[13] Greek organizations function as incubators for student culture—at their best they can foster a value for leadership or community, but at their worst participation is linked with increases in binge drinking, prejudiced racial attitudes, and lower rates of interracial friendship.[14] Organizations are powerful venues in which members can push their peers in one direction or another, making it harder to swim against the current.[15] Yet for whatever reason, fraternities and sororities are rarely named in discussions of who is supposedly self-segregating. Rarely does anyone ask why all of the White students are sitting together in the cafeteria, perhaps because of the way the White majority operates as the default setting for our understanding of what is normal, versus a gathering of students of color, which seems less the norm. These are some of things that get lost—when we're focused on other things.

ETHNIC STUDENT ORGANIZATIONS—SELF-SEGREGATION OR NOT?

There are some surprising research findings out there on the ethnic student organizations that populate college campuses. From a South Asian American acapella group to the local Black Student Union chapter, these groups provide social, academic, and emotional support for their members. They also work to raise awareness on campus about their particular population, often hosting signature events such as a Lunar New Year Celebration or Holi Festival. Such groups are often at the forefront of campus activism, incubating and launching movements to rally for ethnic studies programs and additional support for students of color.

In a more insidious way, these organizations are also often accused of fostering self-segregation, as did the *Georgetown Voice* columnist who lamented how such groups are "counterproductive to the values Georgetown wants to instill."[16] Although that editorial appeared in 2016, public worries around the phenomenon of self-segregation date back to the early 1990s, when headlines warning of "Separate Ethnic Worlds" appeared in the *New York Times*.[17] Reviewing news articles on self-segregation from the past three decades, I uncovered a common theme: the presentation of self-segregation as a catch-all scapegoat for racial problems in higher education. These articles claim that so-called self-segregation is both a symptom and a cause of higher education's deficiencies and that without it college campuses would be the racial utopias they were meant to be. Something tells me that the vision of "racial utopia" held by some of these writers might be pretty different from my own. . . .

Despite the worries around self-segregation fracturing campus life, recent studies indicate counterintuitive findings: involvement in ethnic student organizations is actually linked with significantly *higher* levels of interracial contact and, in particular, the same casual type of interracial contact that is most consistently linked to the educational benefits of diversity.[18] (I'll explain how these benefits come about in a bit.) Being involved in ethnic student organizations is also linked with significantly higher rates of interracial interaction (more casual contact) for students overall, and Black and Latinx students in particular, when analyses are conducted separately by racial/ethnic group. This finding is especially critical to challenging the myth of rampant and static self-segregation, showing that students involved in ethnic student organizations are engaging with the broader diversity of the campus.

In terms of closer types of relationships, research findings also suggest that ethnic student organizations do little to hurt race relations. When simply controlling for any sort of participation in an ethnic student organization, some studies, including my own work, find that these groups are associated with lower odds of having a close friend of another race.[19] Two other types of clubs do as well: Greek life and, surprisingly, religious student organizations, which we'll discuss in the next chapter. However, for students involved in ethnic student organizations, lower rates of closer interracial friendship tend to be accompanied by higher rates of interracial contact, which is a really good thing. Let's break it down.

First, a different story emerges when controlling for the level of involvement in these groups, instead of just indicating membership in these groups. It's a subtle but important difference. Counterintuitively, in a study published in the *Review of Higher Education*, Young K. Kim and I found that being *more* involved in ethnic student organizations had no link with close interracial friendship; there was no negative effect associated with being more involved in an ethnic student organization.[20] However, the negative effect between Greek life and religious student organization membership persisted, meaning that students more involved in fraternities, sororities, and religious groups were significantly less likely to have close friends of other races.

Later on we looked at patterns for students of different racial/ethnic groups. This series of studies was one of the very first to test ideas about who is self-segregating using data on actual friendship groups from a national dataset of thousands of college students, instead of a set of hunches or anecdotes. We found that Latinx students who were more involved in ethnic student groups were actually *more* likely to have close friends of other races during college.[21] While the type of statistical method that we used does not prove causality (we cannot say that clubs make or guarantee interracial friendships), Latinx students who were more involved in ethnic student groups actually had significantly more interracial friendships, even when controlling for other key background characteristics. Importantly, for other racial groups, being more involved in ethnic student organizations had no net effect, meaning that students who were more involved were no more likely to have (or not have) close interracial friendships. While results that are statistically significant are usually the ones that receive the most attention, sometimes a lack of statistical significance is just as noteworthy, especially when it contradicts conventional wisdom about a potential relationship between two variables. In this case, the finding that more involvement in ethnic student organizations had no negative effect on interracial friendship for students is quite remarkable given the reputation of these groups as promoting self-segregation.

These studies on ethnic student groups and close interracial friendships are important, but they consider a very specific outcome that has some limitations: the racial/ethnic composition of one's four closest friends. Altogether the research suggests that we derive more benefits from interacting continuously within a broader network of diverse peers than simply having a limited number of closer interracial friendships.[22] While our most intimate friendships are important (after all, is there anything like someone who knew how weird you were in high school?), we know that in regular life we often rely on a variety of networks that extend beyond our "big four." When we rely on only our closest friendships for news and information, there is a high likelihood that we will hear the same information over and over again. Ultimately, it becomes less novel and less likely to make you look at the world in a totally different way. However, interracial interaction among a broader network of diverse acquaintances and friends—the kind linked with participation in ethnic student organizations—is especially valuable because these networks can open the door to a catalyzing agent in cognitive development: nonredundant information.[23] Even a close interracial friendship, life-impacting as it may be, represents an n of 1. Having one Asian American friend may enlighten you to some of the challenges of the model minority myth, or the "bamboo ceiling"; but having more Asian American friends might show you that a lot of Asian Americans don't go to college or attend community college.[24] You might be pushed to consider why many Asian Americans identify as Democrat and others as Republican, and even the few who are holding it down with the Green Party. You would learn about Asian Americans who grow up in refugee families versus those whose parents signed up to come over. You'd hear the perspective of the Asian American who was the prom queen, the class clown, the animal lover, the car whiz. You get the idea. Add in friendships and acquaintanceships from other racial/ethnic groups and other backgrounds, and you get a fuller understanding of how people are experiencing life.

SO WHY DOES INTERRACIAL INTERACTION MATTER?

To elaborate, with a broader network of interracial interactions we get exposed to sources that can challenge our thinking and help us reconsider preconceived notions. This exact pattern is a huge reason why racial diversity in college campuses matters and how the educational benefits associated with diversity work. Navigating modern life takes a tremendous amount of effort, and most of us spend our day on autopilot to conserve mental energy. Psychologist Ellen Langer called this state "mindlessness," and, frankly, we're in it a lot.[25] Our brains rely on mental shortcuts (like the availability heuristic, for instance) to help us make sense of the world. On top of that, we are socialized in a world to identify patterns and associate them with various people, groups, or situations, which leads to the persistence of stereotypes, both the supposedly positive ones and the more unkind ones. These patterns and assumptions also become part of life on autopilot, as we have to quickly categorize and generalize our observations. It's not all bad, and we need some of it to function. But with too much mindlessness we can miss out.

When we really stop to listen—something that is getting increasingly harder in an age of technology saturation—encountering a nonredundant, novel piece of information can really take us off autopilot. All of a sudden we have to be present and mindful that this new piece of information does not neatly fall into the boxes and silos of our preconceived notions. Our brain has to work a little harder as we digest this information and how it challenges the way we understand the world around us. In young adulthood, these types of encounters spur cognitive development and complexity as young people move from seeing the world in more black-and-white terms typical of earlier stages of development to more gray and contextual, nuanced understandings of the world.[26]

In the college environment, interacting across race has a proven track record of being linked with this type of critical development. In fact, interracial interaction during college has been linked to a wide array of important outcomes like cognitive skills, academic skills, lower rates of prejudice, increased comfort with people of other races, social agency and civic development, retention, sense of belonging, cultural understanding and engagement, leadership and teamwork skills, and satisfaction in college.[27] In the last few Supreme Court affirmative action cases, the Court has ruled repeatedly that universities have a compelling interest in bringing together racially diverse student bodies which foster environments that can spur these types of benefits. This definitely isn't the only justification for affirmative action. The effects of past and current discrimination and disenfranchisement are real, but it is the justification that the Court has preserved as legally viable for now. At the same time, part of why the educational benefits linked with diversity are particularly compelling and critical is because society remains segregated by race, which is the enduring legacy of both past and current discrimination.

WHY DO STUDENTS IN ETHNIC STUDENT ORGANIZATIONS HAVE HIGHER INTERRACIAL INTERACTION?

Good question. It's counterintuitive, given everything we know (or think we know) when it comes to Black, Asian American, or Latinx kids sitting together in the cafeteria. As I mentioned earlier, the cafeteria really only represents a portion of a day that otherwise contains many hours and opportunities to cross paths across racial/ethnic lines. Seeing a large group of Black, Asian American, or Latinx students sitting in a room together for a meeting of ____ (fill in the blank with your favorite ethnic/cultural student club) may also give the impression that ethnic student organizations lead to persistent racial clustering on campus. Yet, those meetings are also just another fraction of a student's day when it comes to campus life.

Part of the reason why ethnic student organizations are linked with higher levels of interracial interaction is that these communities give students of color some space to breathe and recharge, enabling them to go back out and engage across race. Many of these students spend most of their day interacting across race, and research has documented how these experiences can be taxing and depleting in their own way.[28] Students may encounter challenges like racial microaggressions—well-meaning, subtle comments that reinforce their minority status.[29] On top of highlighting stereotypes, racial microaggressions are taxing because they make the hearer question whether they are overreacting or reading too much into the original comment, which can really make you feel crazy over time. Remember, these are usually split-second comments that are well-intentioned. Students may also encounter more blatant acts of racism and ignorance, but more subtle slights can be quite disorienting on their own.

Marginalization can happen for students of color without a word being spoken. Imagine the African American student walking into the engineering classroom where she is the only person of her race. As an Asian American, I am sorely aware of situations where I am the lone (or one of very few) Asian Americans or people of color at a gathering or a meeting. More equitable representation of different racial/ethnic groups does not guarantee a positive environment for diversity, but these environments rarely exist without such representation. In other words, numbers matter. I once heard a comment by Louis Martin-Vega, the dean of the College of Engineering at North Carolina State University and a trailblazer in his own right, about how having more faculty and scientists of color is critical not just to provide role models but to stand as "existence proof." *Existence proof*—his words struck me. When campuses lack racial/ethnic diversity among faculty and administrators, there is a literal lack of existence proof for our students. And the feeling that you don't exist—that no one like you exists in the immediate space you inhabit—can be deeply draining both in the moment and over time.

And then let's not forget the pressure that students of color, women, and other traditionally disenfranchised groups experience when they are one of the few in an environment. The pressure to succeed, counter stereotypes, and show others that you do not fit into their neat assumptions of who you are—all while keeping it real enough to not forget who you are in the first place. This all wears on the spirits of many students of color. For instance, study after study has confirmed the effect of stereotype threat—how the standardized test performance of underrepresented minorities and women are hurt when their social identities are made salient in a negative way.[30] All told, stereotype threat is just one manifestation of the burdens that many students carry in a society saturated by inequality. So doesn't it make sense that students of color could use some space to not have to deal with this stuff 24/7?

Even when interacting across race leads to positive connections—the types of deep conversations where students have "Aha!" light bulb moments as they consider new ways of understanding the world—these interactions still take effort. Remember that the entire idea behind why racial diversity affects cognitive growth is because our default mode of automatic thinking takes very little effort, whereas the effort involved in considering a divergent perspective spurs active learning and development. The upside is that you learn something new; the slight downside is that going off mental cruise control takes effort. However, in an unequal society, the burden is even greater for students of color, who often take on a teaching role. Chances are they inhabit this role on multiple occasions, even within a single day, depending on the campus environment. In contrast, a White or majority-status student can experience some disorientation from inhabiting the learner role or engaging in a complex exchange, but they generally have the privilege of going back to enjoying their majority-status role for the rest of the day. The scenario I have described is purposefully overgeneralized. Of course, there are times when the roles are reversed, or the majority-status student has chosen to engage in displacement more than the average majority student. But the fact remains that even the decision of a majority-status student to align with the minority is a choice, an option—a choice unavailable to students of color in most situations.

So there are more than a few reasons why students of color may value a place to breathe, unwind, and recharge with people who share their racial/ethnic identity. Ethnic student organizations—and yes, sitting together at the cafeteria—can provide those spaces where students do not have to second-guess themselves as much, for at least a period of time.

There still may be plenty of disorienting moments—one should definitely not assume homogeneity within any particular community—but there is something valuable about having times when you don't have to wonder whether the disorientation is stemming from inhabiting the position of "official racial minority."[31]

The exciting thing about spending time with people of the same race/ethnicity is that for college students overall, and Black and Latinx students in particular, being involved in various types of ethnic student organizations is linked with significantly *higher* rates of overall interracial contact. Having time to recharge, socialize, and enjoy fellowship among peers of a similar racial background is associated with higher rates of crossing racial/ethnic lines during the other hours of the day. Ethnic student organizations play a vital role in not just helping retain students of color; they also contribute to the broader campus racial climate by promoting interracial interaction, giving students of color space to recharge their batteries and navigate a diverse and at times racially charged campus environment.[32]

Researchers have identified other positive outcomes from involvement in ethnic student organizations. Rodolfo Mendoza-Denton of the University of California, Berkeley, and Elizabeth Page-Gould of the University of Toronto have conducted a number of studies on the value of interracial friendships.[33] They have also found that

> efforts to foster out-group contact need not come at the expense of promoting the benefits of in-group contact. For example, in a previous study, we . . . demonstrated that on days following attendance at ethnically centered events (e.g., attendance at a meeting of the Black Students' Organization), minority students' sense of belonging at the university increased. Together, the findings of these studies suggest that efforts to increase crossgroup friendship are not incompatible with institutional efforts to clearly communicate acceptance of the minority group by supporting organizations or activities centered on the ethnic or racial background of that group.[34]

Score another point for ethnic student organizations. The authors found that participation in these groups and other ethnically based activities for students of color is actually linked with an increased sense of belonging at the institution, instead of feelings of alienation and isolation. And that's good news for everyone.

WE NEED BOTH *INTER*RACIAL AND *INTRA*RACIAL ENGAGEMENT

One reason why the image of the racially zoned cafeteria (or the ethnic student organization) has imprinted itself on the public's consciousness as an example of what is wrong with diversity is that we have the misguided tendency to think that diversity is an all-or-nothing concept. Well-intentioned people take statements like Martin Luther King Jr.'s "I Have a Dream" speech and uncritically envision a racially mixed society as a static, fixed picture. If pervasive, state-mandated racial segregation was certainly bad, then the opposite—people-chosen 24/7 integration—can only be good. Perhaps we lack the language to think about both the middle ground and the complex processes that support a more diverse society. And without this understanding, when we see some degree of people-chosen congregation along racial/ethnic lines, we jump to conclusions and put it in the same category as state-mandated racial segregation ("bad").

In reality, supporting diversity is a more fluid process in which most individuals benefit from a balance of both intergroup (interracial) interaction and intragroup interaction. One does not necessarily come at the expense of the other, especially for students of color. Interracial interactions among a broad network of friends and acquaintances are critical, both to expose people to a constant flow of nonredundant information (avoiding groupthink) and to support interracial cooperation. They are also crucial for needs like finding a job or getting the word out about your ideas. Mark Granovetter of Stanford University summed up the importance of having a broad network of acquaintanceships in his seminal article "The Strength of Weak Ties."[35] Counterintuitively, he found that successful job contacts are more likely to come from more casual social ties than close friendships, in part because the greater number of casual ties will serve as a source of nonredundant information. Similarly, it is generally fine to have a close-knit network of friends of the same race/ethnicity who can provide emotional support and intimate friendship, as long as students have a broader and more diverse network to advance them in the workplace and other spheres of life. Now more than ever, racially diverse neighborhoods, schools, and communities play a critically foundational role in supporting our country's diverse democracy.

In short, for students of color, spending time with one's own racial/ethnic group is something that may actually help interracial contact in the long run. It seems paradoxical, but when we remember that people have the ability to manage both interracial and intraracial relationships, we realize that these types of relationships are a both-and, not an either-or, trade-off. Since White students tend to have lower rates of casual interracial contact and interracial friendship, it is imperative that universities typify communities where White students engage in environments that do not shelter them from engaging across racial/ethnic lines. While interracial contact is basically unavoidable for students of color in most collegiate settings, White students can more easily opt out of this type of engagement, especially at predominantly White universities. The next chapter presents some of the environments (historically White Greek life) that are shaping these experiences for White students.

CHAPTER TWO

Who's Really Self-Segregating?

Sororities, Fraternities, and Religious Groups

IN THE LAST CHAPTER, we discussed how an environment that seems like a primary culprit in promoting racial divisions on campus—ethnic student organizations—can actually support student engagement across racial/ethnic lines. For Black and Latinx students involved in these groups, research suggests that their intraracial, within-group interactions don't limit their interracial interactions. Yet there are other communities on campus that may prevent students from mixing with the broader racial diversity of the university: Greek letter organizations, particularly predominantly or historically White fraternities and sororities.

So let's take a closer look at who's really self-segregating (if anyone is) on college campuses. And we should also take a look at an environment that is seldom on the radar for diversity educators: religious student organizations. They, too, tend to be primarily composed of one racial/ethnic group and, like Greek letter organizations, are linked with lower rates of close interracial friendship. However, we'll see that, on the whole, students who participate in these groups do seem to be engaging with the broader diversity of the campus, which is a good thing.

GREEK LIFE AND RACE: A CHALLENGING TRACK RECORD

When there are places where spending time with one's racial/ethnic group is *not* accompanied by high interracial contact, campuses should be worried. Participation in Greek life organizations is linked with significantly lower rates of close interracial friendship for White students.[1] In an article published in the *Sociology of Education*, the authors found that "although they begin college with similar proportions of interracial friends, white students who do not join Greek organizations gain proportionately more interracial friendships."[2] In other words, White students who go Greek have even lower levels of interracial friendship during college than their non-Greek peers who are also White. When it comes to more casual interracial contact, however, the findings are mixed. Some studies find no effect while others find significantly lower levels of interacting across races for students active in Greek organizations.[3] It appears that unlike ethnic student organizations, where spending time with one's own racial/ethnic group essentially refuels underrepresented minority (URM) students, enabling them to engage with the broader diversity of the campus, participation in Greek life for White students is either doing nothing (best-case scenario) or hurting their engagement with the diversity of the campus (worst-case scenario).

What worries me are the studies that link participation in Greek life with harmful attitudes and unfortunate outcomes, such as negative attitudes toward interracial marriage, increased opposition to diversity on campus, and higher levels of symbolic racism.[4] To understand why Greek life is associated with negative interracial outcomes, it makes sense to probe the numbers behind these organizations. One problem is that the national Greek life organizations—the National Panhellenic Conference (NPC, sororities) and the Inter-Fraternity Council (IFC, fraternities)—do not track these numbers at a national or chapter level, to my knowledge, although institutions themselves may have the data. I discovered this firsthand as an undergraduate researcher trying to find the racial/ethnic breakdown of the Panhellenic sororities at a local institution I was studying, and the director of Greek Life suggested that we request the information from sorority presidents. Somehow word got out, and this twenty-one-year-old was a little bewildered to get a "cease and desist" letter from the NPC insisting that "none of the member groups of the National Panhellenic Conference ever inquire about the racial/ethnic background of their members. We value the worth of the individual regardless of her racial/ethnic background.[5] It certainly is not a criteria [*sic*] for membership in any one of our organizations. We do not permit our membership lists to be used in demographic studies." A supportive administrator was not deterred, however, and got me the numbers: sorority membership at Southern University (I'll call it) was 88.4 percent White, which seemed high even at a campus that was 82 percent White at the time.[6]

But looking at data from only one institution is limiting. Is there any national data on the racial/ethnic composition of Greek life? After all, it could just be a case of the availability heuristic, where we repeatedly hear about cases of fraternities or sororities engaging in destructive, racially loaded behavior. Think about the Sigma Alpha Epsilon fraternity from the University of Oklahoma, which was caught on video singing a song with the lyrics saying "there will never be a [n-word] in SAE."[7] Or the Alpha Xi Delta sorority at Miami University in Ohio, which somehow thought that it would be a good idea to trash the National Underground Railroad Museum—yes, the museum honoring the Underground Railroad—during its spring formal.[8] Or the racially themed parties that get thrown over and over again, as if different groups are taking turns on rotation ("Alright Phi Alpha Beta, this year you're up to make the headlines, and your options are Ghetto Superstar, South of the Border, or White Trash BBQ—what will it be?"). Is it simply that we hear about exceptional, memorable cases, or are broader, more insidious patterns at work?

We do have one national data source tracking the racial/ethnic composition of these groups for a sample of twenty-eight institutions, the National Longitudinal Study of Freshmen (NLSF). It's not perfect—the institutions run selective (fewer publics) and the data are self-reported based off students' observations—but, still, the information is illuminating and worth looking at. Among participants, 97.1 percent of White students involved in a fraternity or sorority reported being in one that was mostly or almost all White. Latinx students were the group most likely to be involved in a fraternity or sorority that was racially mixed (10.0 percent).[9] Of those Black students involved in Greek life, 55.7 percent indicated membership in majority-Black Greek organizations, presumably groups that are part of the historically Black National Pan-Hellenic Council, and 32.8 percent in predominantly White organizations.

From this snapshot we see the general pattern of Greek letter organizations being the most racially isolating environments for White students and less so for students of color. Interestingly, in two case studies of race and Greek life, one I conducted in the mid-2000s at a private, predominantly White southern institution and another I assisted with at a large public institution in the mid-Atlantic region with a higher degree of racial diversity—a consistent finding was that the most elite sororities were the Whitest in composition.[10] They might have a sprinkling of women of color who were trotted out as mascots ("I know that Tri-Delta has a Black girl"), but the dominant culture of the elite groups was still heavily White. Furthermore, in many cases members were also known for being thin and wealthy and, in general, exemplars of Western standards of beauty. Of the women of color who were active in sororities, most of them tended to join those viewed as less elite or that had some level of accessibility and open-mindedness to women of color, as well as women who might not fit the mold of the elite sororities (e.g., different body types, social classes).

WHY BLAME ETHNIC STUDENT ORGANIZATIONS BUT NOT GREEK LIFE?

Before we talk more about why the demography of Greek life is what it is, it's worth considering why the media frequently calls out ethnic student organizations and students of color eating together in the cafeteria for fostering self-segregation but not these massive one-hundred-plus-person, 95 percent White organizations. Besides our tendency to see White people as the norm, the idea of *selective attention* helps explain why we focus on one group but not the other. Basically, the concept is that it's really hard to focus on two things at a time. In a famous experiment conducted at Harvard, psychology faculty Christopher Chabris and Daniel Simons had participants watch a video about six people passing two basketballs around. Three of the people in the video wore white shirts and the other three black shirts.[11] They instructed participants to keep track of the number of passes made by people wearing white shirts. (Cue the Harlem Globetrotter's theme music.) In the middle of the video, a person in a gorilla suit comes out (yes, a gorilla). The gorilla isn't coy or shy; it takes center stage, thumping its chest and hanging out for a good nine seconds. Amazingly, half of the participants who watched the video totally missed the gorilla.[12] This experiment is a beautifully simple example of how easy it is to miss the literal gorilla in the room when our focus is directed elsewhere.

Now when you go to the cafeteria, you aren't tasked with counting how many times people are throwing a basketball (or cafeteria tray), but something like students of color sitting together still feels notable and perhaps eats up our memory. Arguably, we focus our attention on these things that strike us as unusual and often forget the bigger picture of who else is in the cafeteria or what's going on in other parts of campus. Since our attention is limited and selective, our mental references subsequently default to what is memorable or available—those tables at the cafeteria. It's so easy to recall the times students seem like they aren't mixing across race, or at least some students, that it's easy to miss the times when they are. Similarly, when we fixate on one group that's supposedly fostering the self-segregation, we miss the big gorilla of an entire system that is the majority, especially one that is overwhelmingly White in composition.

#WHYSOWHITE???

When thinking about why certain groups in Greek life remain almost all White in composition, it is important to remember that while NPC/IFC groups do not explicitly cater to a particular race/ethnicity, both groups spent a considerable amount of energy over their respective histories working to keep people of color out. Since their early days, fraternities and sororities had official, formal exclusionary policies barring people of color (and, in numerous cases, non-Christians) from membership. There were real "discriminatory clauses against Negroes and Orientals" in place, and the political and historical dynamics behind them are fascinating.[13] In the mid–twentieth century, the official policies shifted, and by 1955 only one NPC sorority had an official ban on students of color. Still—surprise surprise—as midcentury observer Alfred McClung Lee observed in *Fraternities Without Brotherhood*, a real gem chronicling this history, the NPC and IFC groups remained as racially homogeneous (lily White) as ever: there was no more need for a formal policy, since the message had already been sent, loud and clear, about who was welcome and who was not. Fast-forward many decades later, and we see that racial/ethnic divides persist in Greek life, even though diversity on college campuses has increased and no IFC or NPC organization maintains any sort of formal exclusionary policy. Why is this?

One might argue that the divides are due to the founding and continuation of Greek life groups catering to different racial/ethnic minorities, some of which were founded because students of color had been officially excluded from mainstream groups. It's a "blame the minorities" argument. There's a similar parallel in the rhetoric which claims that college campuses would be racial utopias if it were not for those pesky students of color wanting to eat in the cafeteria together. While the groups that encompass multicultural Greek life (e.g., Asian American, Latinx, and multicultural-interest fraternities and sororities) and the National Pan-Hellenic Council (the nine historically African American groups) thrive on many campuses, their numbers tend to be smaller. Available data from the NLSF confirm this: out of Black, Latinx, and Asian American students involved in Greek life, only 55.7 percent of Black students, 14.4 percent of Latinx, and 18.9 percent of Asian American students were actually involved in fraternities or sororities that were "mostly Black," "mostly Latino/a," and "mostly Asian" in composition, respectively.[14] Even when accounting for the students of color who join ethnic-specific Greek letter organizations, plenty of students of color could potentially join the mainstream IFC/NPC groups but do not. And among the students of color who do join Greek life, a good percentage participate in historically and predominantly White groups, countering the misperception that Greek life remains White because students of color only join groups specifically catering to students of color.[15] The historically White groups remain mostly White because not many students of color join Greek life, period.

The case of racial homogeneity—basically concentrated Whiteness—persisting in historically White Greek life (HWGL), even on more racially diverse campuses is a real concern given that participation in these groups is linked with negative outcomes like symbolic racism, racist attitudes, and lower interracial contact.[16] I am a hopeless believer in (some of) the goodness of humanity and sincerely hope that very few people actually want Greek life to be this way. Of course, some do. I mean, fraternity members really thought it was okay to sing a song called "There Will Never Be a [N-Word] in SAE"—until they were exposed in the national media in 2015. But terrible people aside, how do you explain the persistence of racial homogeneity in the absence of explicit policies that seek to exclude students of color? Or, as brilliantly phrased by sociologist Eduardo Bonilla-Silva, how do you have racism (or persistent racial divides) without racists?[17] It's a compelling, $64,000 question that does not have a single answer.

In part, the case of persistent racial homogeneity in HWGL speaks to the power of historical legacies of exclusion on the campus racial climate, as documented in the framework proposed by Sylvia Hurtado, Jeffrey Milem, Alma Clayton-Pederson, and Walter Allen.[18] Their original framework proposes four interlocking elements of climate: (1) the historical legacies of exclusion of college campuses, (2) the racial/ethnic composition of the campus (and various subcultures), (3) inter- and intragroup relations, and (4) the psychological dimension of climate—how do people feel, experience, and perceive it? While Hurtado and colleagues' framework is generally applied to universities as a whole, it also serves to understand climate issues in subsections of the university, such as HWGL. Arguably, the four dimensions as applied to HWGL tend to reinforce an organizational culture and climate that is largely inhospitable to many students of color, although some do choose to participate. The campus racial climate framework speaks to the significance of historical legacies of exclusion, the decades and decades of explicit bans on students of color in HWGL. Even when such bans were lifted, they left behind an unspoken legacy of who was welcome or not in these organizations. And while their power has loosened somewhat over the years (with some groups diversifying and other, more elite groups usually having at least one token student of color or a sprinkling of diversity), they still have such a deep legacy that some HWGL groups have pretty much the same racial/ethnic composition they had fifty or seventy-five years ago.

Another issue is that most HWGL groups have a basic organizational culture of color blindness. The line of thinking goes that the official bans against students of color ("the bad days") were lifted many years ago and are in the past, thus HWGL organizations have no reason or responsibility to address the usually unspoken role of race within the system. In my own research, I found that women of color who joined HWGL groups (Asian Americans, specifically) spoke indirectly about ways that race mattered in HWGL. They talked about feeling unwelcome at recruitment events for certain sororities, observing how elite sororities tend to be more White, and experiencing racial microaggressions. Still, they were extremely hesitant to label such incidents as having anything to do with race. In their minds, anything having to do with race was tantamount to racism (perpetuated by racists), and their "sisters" and community were not racist. Therefore, race was irrelevant, and they had no language to talk about it, especially for situations that weren't blatantly racist but where race still mattered.

If this dynamic existed among the women of color in HWGL groups, you can only imagine how common it might be among the broader, majority-White membership, except with less recognition of incidents like racial microaggressions and the like. All of this goes to say that HWGL has a problem but few tools to diagnose and address it openly. Racial issues are framed as things of the past (e.g., historical exclusionary policies) or linked only to incidents with blatant acts of racism, leaving students and leaders without the language needed to understand how (1) the past affects the present and (2) how race can have a powerful influence on organizational culture without anyone (or most people) having a bad, racist heart.

RACIAL AND SOCIOECONOMIC DIVERSITY: BUFFERING THE NEGATIVE EFFECTS OF GREEK LIFE

There is one broader, institutional dynamic that can help alleviate the racial divides that are rampant within this system: the presence of structural racial diversity in an institution. With *structural racial diversity* I am referring to the basic racial/ethnic composition of a student body and, more specifically, the level of racial heterogeneity in a student body. How diverse is it, and is that diversity coming from multiple racial/ethnic groups?

While study after study has found a negative link between Greek life participation and interracial friendship, in a study Young K. Kim and I published in the *Review of Higher Education* we found that the negative relationship between being active in Greek life and having friends of other races was lessened by attending a more racially diverse institution.[19] In other words, the negative outcome normally linked with Greek life—having fewer interracial friendships—was less apparent for fraternity and sorority members who attended more diverse colleges and universities. We suggest that such institutions have many students of different race/ethnicities, so interacting across race is not as easily avoidable as it might be at a more homogeneous institution. In these cases, Greek life functions less as a force field that shelters students from the diversity of the institution than it might at other, less diverse institutions. Another thought is that HWGL might be a less dominant force at highly diverse institutions, having less of a monopoly on social life. Participants may be more active in other spheres of campus, beyond Greek life. And, hopefully, at more diverse institutions HWGL itself will be more diverse: while it might still be a majority-White system, it might have more diversity than if it existed at a more homogeneous institution.

Anecdotally, I have seen such configurations at institutions like MIT, Harvard, and the University of California, Riverside, where HWGL tends to have a greater degree of racial/ethnic diversity. Yet, in speaking with a former staff member of Greek life at the University of California, Berkeley, I was amazed to hear them lament the lack of diversity within the HWGL system there, a reminder that racial diversity at the institutional level does not guarantee it will trickle down to various subcultures of the student body.

Socioeconomic diversity within racial/ethnic groups is also an important part of diluting some of the negative effects linked with HWGL. *When combined* with racial diversity, socioeconomic diversity challenges the consolidation of privilege along both racial and economic lines.[20] Part of why HWGL sororities and fraternities can shield their members from engaging with the broader diversity of the campus is because they represent not just the consolidation of students along racial lines (predominantly White groups) but, in many cases, the consolidation of students along boundaries that are both racial and socioeconomic. So an elite sorority or fraternity is dominated by not just White students but by White wealthy students, thereby strengthening racial boundaries. Some might argue that it's really just a social class boundary that makes Greek life divisive, but what we really have at work is intersectionality; racial boundaries are combined and reinforced with economic ones. Arguably, the Greek life organization that has more socioeconomic diversity among a predominantly White membership tends to attract more students of color. I found this in my own research: Asian American women tended to join less elite sororities, which also happened to be more socioeconomically diverse.[21] So adding socioeconomic diversity to the mix—for students of color and White students—can challenge this balkanization that is stronger when racial lines are reinforced by socioeconomic privilege.

Indeed, there are no easy answers to the racial divisions in HWGL. My preference would be to just end HWGL altogether, because all too often the bad outweighs the good, and the good that does come out of these groups (e.g., building community, fostering leadership) can be replicated through other initiatives that don't seem to lend themselves to destructive behaviors. But for educators and institutions that decide to preserve it, I offer these minimum recommendations.

- *Recognize that the past legacy of exclusion in HWGL affects the present, and don't skirt it.* If you care about student development and student learning, address the past head-on and don't dismiss it as irrelevant to current times. Sometimes it takes addressing the ugly to open the door for a better future.
- *Examine what language students are using to talk about race and racial homogeneity.* Is race automatically equated with racism? Help students develop a stronger literacy and fluency around understanding race and its significance. And it's not all bad. Recognizing race/ethnicity can be a beautiful thing.

- *Build opportunities for cross-racial engagement.* Collaborate and support events held by ethnic student organizations; cohost events with NPHC and other ethnic-interest Greek life organizations. Don't let Greek life be a force field that prevents students from engaging with the broader diversity of the campus. There is no quick fix to change these groups. But at minimum, creating opportunities so HWGL groups aren't shielded from the diversity of the campus is critical.

RACE IN SURPRISING PLACES: RELIGIOUS STUDENT ORGANIZATIONS

One other type of student organization that shapes the campus racial climate in surprising ways is religious student organizations. Yes, religion. We're used to thinking of religion playing a polarizing role due to other dynamics—those who see religion as important versus those who do not, members of various faith traditions disagreeing with how you get to some manifestation of the afterlife—but rarely do we include religion in our discussions of racial dynamics with college students.

I came to this research topic by surprise. When I was in graduate school on the West Coast, I noticed that the majority of Christian evangelical groups (commonly referred to as "campus fellowships") were divided along racial lines: they either had a majority-White membership or were made up of Asian American students. The proliferation of Asian American campus fellowships at universities has been a fascination among some sociologists and anthropologists. By some estimates, places like UCLA are home to as many twenty to thirty such groups, from the Asian American Christian Fellowship to the Korean Bible Study. While some cater to immigrant students who prefer to worship and socialize in their native language, the majority operate in English and serve second-plus-generation Asian Americans. To be sure, Asian Americans are not the only ones who cluster within their race/ethnicity. The research of Rebecca Kim, a sociologist at Pepperdine University, tracked these groups at UCLA, where she observed how White students gravitated toward the Campus Crusade for Christ chapter, as it became the unofficial hub for White evangelicals there. At the same time, she explained that Asian American campus fellowships proliferated partly because of the subtle exclusion that students felt from majority-White spaces like Campus Crusade. In turn, the Asian American campus fellowships provided a sense of belonging and a way to make a very big campus feel a little smaller.

Of course, the intersection between race and religion is not limited to college. A popular saying attributed to Martin Luther King Jr. reminds that "Sunday is the most segregated time of the week." The African American church arose from the literal exclusion of Blacks from White churches from the time of slavery. Immigrant religious communities catering to newcomers from across the world are often bedrock civic institutions, providing a space where newer arrivals can speak their native language and receive valuable social support.[22] Mosques, temples, churches, and synagogues are all places where people come to "do life" alongside each other, creating community in a fractured world. To note, though, national data suggest that only around 14 percent of religious institutions can be categorized as multiracial.[23]

And these are the worlds that many of our college students grow up in. The Spirituality in Higher Education Project, a national study of college students run out of the UCLA Higher Education Research Institute, found that 79 percent of first-year students surveyed reported believing in God and 81 percent had attended religious services occasionally or frequently during their senior year of high school.[24] While many students walk away from religion during college, the fact remains that a significant proportion receives some sort of socialization in a religious community that is likely racially homogeneous prior to college. Some students who grow up in a community that specifically caters to a particular racial/ethnic group (e.g., historically Black congregations) might be aware that their religious upbringing had an influence on their experiences with race, or the formation of a racial/ethnic identity. But White students who are used to making up the majority presence may have little idea of this dynamic, just as members of a HWGL group might see themselves as "normal" versus the way they view the existence of a historically Black group.

Are racially homogeneous religious communities just limited to a few campuses, or are they part of a broader phenomenon? To answer this question, we need data. The same National Longitudinal Study of Freshmen that tracked the racial/ethnic composition of Greek letter organizations also did the same for religious student organizations. For White students who indicated participation, 81.4 percent claimed that they participated in religious groups that were majority White in composition. Of Black students, a smaller 57.7 percent indicated participating in a majority-Black student religious group. No Latinx students indicated participating in a majority-Latinx religious student organization, possibly because a high percentage of Latinx students affiliate as Catholic, and Catholic campus communities are less likely to cater to a particular racial/ethnic group. Latinx students were also most likely to participate in religious groups that could be characterized as biracial or multiracial in composition (15.4 percent). And 69.2 percent of Asian Americans active in religious student groups participated in one that was majority Asian American, which seems high but also could be seen as lower than expected for people who have spent time observing the strong presence of such groups on the West Coast in particular. Interestingly, 10.3 percent of Black students and 11.5 percent of Latinx students active in religious groups reported participating in organizations that had a majority Asian American membership, indicating an opportunity for crossing racial/ethnic boundaries.[25]

Participation in campus religious groups that have a majority presence of a particular racial/ethnic group is a trend for White, Asian American, and African Americans. But do these patterns have any relationship with actual behavior? In a series of studies, colleagues and I found that religious student organization participation was linked with significantly lower levels of close interracial friendship, even when controlling for race/ethnicity and other key background characteristics.[26] Even when we controlled for actual involvement in such groups, versus mere affiliation, students active in religious groups were less likely to have close interracial friendships. Also, this pattern existed regardless of potential mediating factors like the racial diversity of the campus.

However, religious student groups and students who identify as religious have their own quirky dynamics. While participation in groups is linked with fewer close interracial friendships, we found, using a national dataset, that students who identified as more religious actually had significantly higher rates of interracial interaction—that is, their interactions across race with a broader network of friends and acquaintances.[27] Interracial interaction was also greater for students from religious minority backgrounds (e.g., Hindu, Buddhist), regardless of the race/ethnicity of the student. And, last, participation in those same campus religious groups linked with lower close interracial friendship is statistically unrelated to general interracial interaction. Even when the study controlled for involvement in a racially homogeneous campus religious group (how wonderful to have data to do this!), we found no net effect on interracial interaction.

Like ethnic student organizations, religious student groups provide another example of communities which harbor close same-race friendships, but generally don't prevent students from interacting with the broader diversity of the campus. Perhaps even more so than ethnic student organizations, religious student organizations are a natural environment in which to nurture close relationships. Students bond over a shared religious identity, often banding together on campuses that feel less than receptive to religiosity. Scholars like Paul Bramadat, Peter Magolda, and Alyssa Rockenbach have all described the intense, close-knit relationships that can come out of such subcultures.[28] Given that the broader landscape of religion in the United States is heavily divided by race, forming close friendships with people from the same religious community often lends itself to forming close friendships with same-race peers—both for Whites and students of color. For students of color in particular, such groups can foster a sort of ethno-religious identity where the lines between what it means to be of a particular race/ethnicity and what it means to be of a particular faith tradition become blurred.[29] This dynamic probably goes on for Whites as well, but in a more implicit fashion, since Whiteness is viewed as normative, the default option. As long as students are still interacting across race and experiencing some level of cognitive challenge from engaging with difference, there is little harm with religion writ large when it comes to campus race relations.

Of course, there are still reasons to be cautious of religious groups. While they can spur significant growth and development, campus faith-based organizations can also shield students from grappling with difficult questions.[30] On this point, however, I have documented the innovative practices used to spur serious conversations about race and meaningful interracial friendships that happen in the rare religious organizations that are multiracial in composition.[31] It doesn't always happen, but when it does, faith identity can be a way to engage students on critical social issues, such as racial/ethnic identity, police brutality, sustainability, and the like. I remember encouraging a religiously and politically conservative Christian friend to take a women's studies class because, hey, didn't Jesus care about women? Although he was resistant, eventually he let me pick "just one class" for him to take. On my recommendation, he took the popular Seminar on Gender and Violence, taught at Vanderbilt University by the amazing and inspirational Alison Piepmeier—and yes, his world was turned upside down.

Just as there is no need to abolish ethnic student organizations for promoting so-called self-segregation, there is nothing problematic about a religious student organization catering to students of color. In the name of religious unity, there has been an impetus to diversify both religious institutions in general society and on college campuses, which has some positive motivations and outcomes. But researchers like Korie Edwards of the Ohio State University have shown that racially integrated religious communities can unknowingly reinforce their own forms of White privilege and supremacy, reflecting how "diversity" can be done poorly.[32] Religious organizations that provide a forum for students of color to challenge racial isolation, as well as some breathing room from the day-to-day bustle of campus life and the draining effect of interacting across race all day, can play a positive role in the campus racial climate, and existing research suggests that these groups do not preclude students of color from engaging with the broader diversity of the campus.

However, campus educators should pay attention to majority-race students who are active in religious communities that reflect the same racial/ethnic makeup. Are these students, who are more easily able to opt out of interacting across race, receiving the challenge that they need? Like Greek life communities, religious student groups can also be guilty of promoting a culture of color blindness wherein "race doesn't matter" due to the lack of formal exclusionary policies.[33] Despite having no easy answers and one-size-fits-all solutions, educators must be sensitive to the landscape and dynamics of their own institutions. For both Greek life and religious student life, there may be opportunities to encourage students from different groups to collaborate across racial/ethnic lines on opportunities like community service, intermural sports, or service-learning projects. Both types of groups could also benefit from awkward but necessary conversations on how race may more subtly influence the dynamics of who feels welcome or unwelcome in their communities.

BACK TO THE CAFETERIA

My time at different institutions has shown me that not all cafeterias are alike. In 2011 I moved from teaching at Miami University in rural Ohio to the University of Maryland, College Park (UMD), which is part of the greater Washington, DC, region. While getting to know the offerings in UMD's Stamp Student Union food court, I spent a good amount of time standing in line and people-watching. It was obvious to me from the beginning that the general makeup of that food court was like night and day in comparison to the general flow of the food court at Miami, an institution that was about 80 percent White at the time. Seeing a student of color at UMD was not an aberration but part of the norm. And yes, I did see tables of Asian American kids sitting together, Black kids sitting together, White kids sitting together, and the like. There were also plenty of tables where there was no single racial/ethnic group, or where smaller clusters of students of different races—twos and threes—were eating together.

But what delighted me more than anything was seeing, time and time again, a table of, say, South Asian American students sitting together. And then a Black student would walk up and greet the students sitting there—and then he'd stay to chat. And maybe a White kid would walk up and start talking to another group of students at the same table, and then some of the original sitters would get up and cross over to other tables, and so on. I saw this over and over—times when a student of another race walked up to a table that was all too easily seen as a "Black table" or an "Asian table" to strike up a conversation, compare notes, or laugh boisterously.

Don't get me wrong, UMD has its share of issues related to race. But there is something more fluid about its cafeteria than others I've seen at institutions with less compositional diversity, particularly those with a blaringly White majority. Likewise, when groups like ethnic student organizations and religious student organizations exist at more racially diverse institutions, the evidence suggests that they function in this same way: they spend an hour or so catching up and exhaling before going out into the broader diversity of the institution or, sometimes, inviting that diversity to drop by their cafeteria table. Studies indicate that when these groups exist in an environment that has plenty of opportunities for student interaction across race, they are actually linked with higher rates of cross-racial interaction, which is a really good thing.

Greek life is a bit of a different story. Research indicates that when Greek life organizations exist at more diverse institutions, the net negative impact on interracial friendship is at least blunted. At the same time,

Greek life culture often coexists with destructive norms related to alcohol abuse, sexual assault, and straight-up, blatant racism. At minimum, a racially diverse campus should be a precondition for Greek life organizations to exist; otherwise, the reinforcing effect of "a White bubble within a White bubble" is doing a major disservice to students. However, it's noteworthy that some of the negative effects identified with Greek life participation in the previous study by Jim Sidanius and colleagues—that participating in Greek life was linked to higher levels of symbolic racism and attitudes like opposition to interracial marriage by the fourth year of college—happened at UCLA, "a major, multiethnic university."[34] All of this is to say that Greek life still appears to have some deleterious effects on race relations and student development *even* at more diverse campuses.

There are no easy answers, to be sure, but a hallmark of a healthy campus climate is that it allows continuous self-examination. What groups are contributing to a healthy climate for interracial engagement, and how? The cafeteria can tell us a lot, but, at the same time, it's important to look beyond the couple of hours spent there to see how students are using the rest of the day to interact, learn, and engage—both within and among their own communities.

CHAPTER THREE

Is Class-Based Affirmative Action the Answer?

I REMEMBER CHECKING OUT *The Remedy: Class, Race, and Affirmative Action* during graduate school. It sounded so good. In its pages, Richard Kahlenberg promised readers a simple solution to the equity issues that plague US higher education.[1] To him, a race-conscious admissions process was unnecessarily divisive, violating many people's ideas around what was fair and equitable. But class-based admissions? Smooth like butter. Folks across the political spectrum supported it, even those who stalwartly opposed the version of affirmative action that takes race into account. It was a simple formula: a large percentage of people of color qualify as being low-income; give them a bump up in admissions, and you'll get a twofer—racial diversity without the mess and economic diversity to boot. What's not to like?

Fast-forward two decades and Kahlenberg is having a moment. With race-conscious admissions cases going to the Supreme Court twice in recent years, the public has been more open to his ideas, perhaps feeling that the demise of race-conscious admissions was inevitable. (Spoiler: It wasn't.) Kahlenberg has also been joined by reputable scholars like Sheryll Cashin, who has written about the potential of using zip codes and other data to assess an applicant's opportunity to achieve and the limitations of considering race.[2] But something else happened that made the basic idea of class-based affirmative action a fighting contender again. Malia Obama.

In 2008, the United States made history when we elected Barack Obama to the presidency. It was a shining moment for our democracy. One of Obama's most attractive features was his family, his wife, Michelle, and two daughters, Malia and Sasha. The election of President Obama, writ large, provided fuel to the idea that we were somehow now a postracial society, a claim that exploded in the years to come with Trump and his words about Mexicans and Muslims, Charlottesville and the rise of White supremacy, the BlackLivesMatter movement spotlighting police violence, and the list goes on. But to many, putting a Black family in the White House in 2008 seemed to declare that the problem of racial inequality was now solved—a perfect example of confirmation bias, or interpreting information in a way that confirms what you believe already, if there ever was one.

With that, Malia Obama became a symbol in the affirmative action debates on why race-conscious admissions practices were no longer needed. As *Atlantic* columnist Conor Friedersdorf wrote in 2011, "The notion of advantaged people like Sasha and Malia Obama benefiting from racial preferences is a much better argument against the policy than the experience of their father."[3] In this line of thinking, someone of Barack or Michelle Obama's generation had some legitimacy toward benefiting from affirmative action, as both came from working-class families. But "advantaged people" like the Obamas' children? Since they have it made in the shade, they are prime evidence of why the utility of race-conscious admissions is long over.

Now, I don't doubt that the Obama daughters lead really great lives, benefiting from both the abundant love of their parents and the material advantages that come from having been a First Family. But I do have a problem with the Obama daughters, and Malia in particular (since she was the first to go to college), becoming emblematic of *every* Black girl in America applying to college. Folks like Friedersdorf might challenge this, arguing that they only mean that "advantaged people" who *also happen to be Black* should be out of the running for affirmative action. But there are key problems with that line of thinking.

Number 1, we have no way of knowing who "gets in" via affirmative action, and the idea that all students of color are attending their respective colleges due to affirmative action is erroneous. Affirmative action isn't something that's sprinkled indiscriminately on students of color—"You're Black! Let's give you some admissions fairy dust!" On the contrary, affirmative action is a system of holistic admissions that allows reviewers to assess every single applicant as an individual person with an array of traits—personality, accomplishments, life opportunity, goals, leadership potential, social class, and, yes, race/ethnicity. That includes White students, Black students, Asian American students, Latinx students, Indigenous students, multiracial students. And defenders of race-conscious, holistic admissions maintain that yes, in a country where race/ethnicity is a critical determinant of everything from what type of school you attend to the likelihood that you received SAT coaching to whether you have a higher chance of getting harassed by the police, knowing a student's race/ethnicity is part of being able to assess a student's opportunities for achievement, as well as their broader life story.

Number 2, a wake-up call: the median African American family has 6 percent of the accumulated wealth (assets, savings, property, income) that the median White family has.[4] Six percent. And it's 8 percent for Latinx families. Demos, the think tank that researched this, crunched numbers from the US Census Bureau and found that within each respective community, the median Black household had $7,113 in wealth in 2011. It was $8,348 for the median Latino/a household. The median household wealth for Whites was $111,146. Yes, those are medians—for those of you who slept through stats class, that's the cut-off point for 50 percent of the population. In other words, it's not the crazy 1 percent that's tipping the average for Whites. It's the median figure, $111,146. So $7,113 *versus* $111,146! (Did you drop this book after you read that? Let me give you a minute to find your place again and absorb this information.) Even though I've heard these statistics a million times, the shock value never gets old, especially in a country where people eagerly point to the Obamas and think that racial inequality is a thing of the past.

When it comes to assessing advantage versus disadvantage in an applicant, many URM students have situations that either veer toward some level of relative disadvantage or are less clear cut than being the daughter of the president of the United States. But let's not forget that the Obamas were still paying off student loans right before they landed in the White House. (I'm pretty sure that wasn't the case for any of the Trumps) Yearly income versus accumulated wealth varies dramatically for African American versus Whites in this country due to decades and decades of systemic discrimination against Black people that affected whether they were able to buy property and the value of that property. One word: redlining. The foreclosure crisis, which disproportionately affected URM families, is a reminder of how fragile first-generation wealth or assets are for many people of color.

SO WHY NOT BAN RACE TO HELP LOW-INCOME MINORITIES?

Let me play devil's advocate. Couldn't this all be evidence that class-based affirmative action really is the best solution? In this line of thinking, the stunning Black-Brown-White wealth gap means that low-income URM students—along with low-income Whites who also need a leg up—will stand out and receive the special consideration they deserve. People might think that the race-conscious system does little to help low-income students and that low-income URMs get bumped out by their wealthy peers from minority backgrounds (e.g., Malia Obama). Or that race-conscious affirmative action is the reason for why we have this entire rampant class inequality in higher education, with, in the country's most selective institutions, 74 percent of students coming from the top quartile of income and only 3 percent from the bottom quartile.[5]

It's seductive logic. It's also wrong.

First, the current system already gives weight to social class for low-income URM students. A study conducted by Thomas Espenshade and Alexandria Walton Radford found that private institutions give considerable preference to low-income African American, Latinx, and Asian American applicants. (Yes, Asian Americans—they do benefit!) Could they give more? Probably. But the idea that race-conscious and class-conscious approaches are mutually exclusive is false. Espenshade and Radford found that "Black applicants who come from lower- or working-class families can expect a favorable admissions decision in 87 percent and 53 percent of their cases, respectively. The expected chance of being admitted falls to just 17 percent for upper-class black students. Strikingly similar patterns characterize the admissions chances by social class for Hispanic and Asian applicants to private institutions."[6]

While this finding is probably not going to change the mind of anyone who believes that race is irrelevant to life opportunities, it clearly challenges the idea that the current, race-conscious system helps only wealthy applicants of color. In reality, the opposite is true: affirmative action helps low-income students of color at private institutions. The issue of why low-income students are still underrepresented at elite institutions extends beyond the point of admissions and taps into the makeup of the applicant pool, inequities in college access, and the complexities that influence college choice.

Could there still be more low-income students of all races/ethnicities attending elite institutions? Absolutely. But eliminating consideration of race is not the way to get there. Institutions can and should address both race and class to boost opportunities for low-income students of color.

THE RACIAL WEALTH GAP: WHEN RACE AND CLASS COLLIDE

Claims that the African American student population is disproportionately "advantaged" also ignore the influence of the wealth gap in assessing the life opportunities and experiences of Black students in K–12 education. One example of this claim appears in the Jack Kent Cooke Foundation's (JKCF) report *True Merit: Ensuring Our Brightest Students Have Access to Our Best Colleges and Universities*."[7] I deeply admire the work of JKCF, which has worked aggressively to provide exceptional opportunities for high-achieving, low-income students. I have seen their staff go above and beyond the call of duty to make sure that their scholars have the resources and support to do great things. But while the *True Merit* report highlights important objectives for expanding opportunity for low-income students, throughout it there are subtle digs against race-conscious admissions—which makes sense given that Richard Kahlenberg, who's been beating the drum for class-based affirmative action for the last two decades, is a coauthor. For example, in its commentary on race-conscious admissions, the report states: "As more minority families successfully break through segregated glass ceilings and establish themselves in the middle and upper classes, it is increasingly their children who gain admittance to selective institutions, not the children of minorities living in impoverished, underprivileged neighborhoods. Indeed, 86 percent of Black students at selective colleges are middle or upper-class. This was far from the original intention of race-conscious affirmative action in college admissions."[8] This rhetoric is similar to Friedersdorf's, the suggestion that race-conscious admissions used to have its place (perhaps when society was more blatantly racist) but now works to favor the advantaged.

So let's unpack that statistic of 86 percent of Black students at elite institutions supposedly being middle or upper class. Tracing the footnotes, the original source is William G. Bowen and Derek Bok's classic *The Shape of the River: Long-Term Consequences of Considering Race in College Admissions*, a key piece of evidence supporting the long-term success of race-conscious admissions.[9] Yes, it is ironic that Bowen and Bok's text is being used to argue that race-conscious admissions has lost its "original intention." Looking at the table cited by the report, it appears that the 86 percent figure is a strategic cherry-picking and collapsing of statistics. Bowen and Bok provide three ways to categorize being from a low socioeconomic status background in their sample of students from elite universities. The first criterion is the percentage of students who are first-generation college students; neither parent has a bachelor's degree. Here, Black students outnumber White students more than 2 to 1 (36 percent vs. 15 percent). The second criterion is being from a low-income household (under $22,000 in 1989, the year of data collection). Once again, Black students in the sample are much more likely (20 percent) to come from a low-income background as compared to the White students (3 percent). Let me repeat: Black students are *six times more likely* to come from a low-income background than White students. The last criterion is the percentage of students who meet both of the other criteria—are both first-generation college students *and* from low-income households. It is from this category that the JKCF report pulls the 86 percent statistic, since only 14 percent of Black students in Bowen and Bok's study meet this third criterion. Conveniently, the report seems to miss that only 2 percent of White students are also both first-generation students and from low-income households, which means that Black students are *seven times more likely* to come from a low socioeconomic background than White students.

Saying that 86 percent of Black students in Bowen and Bok's study come from middle or high socioeconomic statuses is technically correct, but it omits the context of how the percentage of Black students who are first-generation students outnumbers the percentage of White first-generation students more than 2 to 1 and how a full 20 percent of Black students at elite schools come from low-income backgrounds, versus only 3 percent of White students. The other problematic issue is the collapsing of middle-SES and high-SES categories to get to that 86 percent. According to Bowen and Bok's analysis, a full 71 percent of Black students come from families that can be classified as middle class, and only 15 percent come from families that are considered upper class. In contrast, only 54 percent of White students come from middle-class families, and a whopping 44 percent come from upper-class families. So yes, White students are three times more likely than Black students to come from high-income families. But those aren't the numbers that you hear, because in the JCKF report categories are collapsed in a way that masks the educational and income disparities between Black and White students at elite institutions.

Contrary to popular belief, statistics on their own do not lie—unless, of course, you blatantly make them up. There are, however, ways of presenting statistics that are misleading, and combining the numbers for middle- and upper-income Black students definitely has that result. It also ignores the context of the racial wealth gap, where the assets (e.g., property, generational wealth) of a middle-class Black family are likely significantly less than those of a middle-class White family. Comparing yearly income to yearly income to gauge who is advantaged or disadvantaged falls short when we know that the average Black family has 6 percent of the overall wealth of the average White family.

Much more than income makes up the complex portrait of social class. Knowing this, it makes sense to not ditch consideration of race in favor of class alone but, instead, to allow institutions to continue to consider *both* in order to capture the unique intersectionality that affects people of color. Let institutions evaluate students on an individual basis with as much available information as possible, examining their achievements and experiences in the context from which they come.

WHY DO PEOPLE OVERESTIMATE BLACK WEALTH?

Before diving into more data, we need to make a quick detour to look at research on cognitive bias to better understand why people underestimate the extent of socioeconomic disadvantage that operates along racial/ethnic lines. In other words, why are some people hung up on thinking that race-conscious admissions is the devil? I gave the Malia Obama example, so now let's think about the principles behind why our brains take that particular mental shortcut.

We could think back to the concept of the availability heuristic, where we can mentally summon Malia Obama as an easily recallable example of Black economic and educational achievement. In turn, when people claim that the racial equity gap pales in comparison to the economic one, we think, "Oh yeah, the Obamas, they're doing great!" Let's not forget that the Obamas are memorable—they're the only non-White First Family in American history—and so their success sticks in our brain to bolster the messaging that (supposedly) "minorities are doing just fine."

Another possible explanation is the concept of *anchoring*, the brain's way of overweighing certain information when making decisions, which is often the first piece of information that a person has learned about a particular subject and what they come to rely on. In other words, we get anchored into thinking that something is the way that it is, making it hard to look beyond that. In everyday life, anchoring can make us overvalue or undervalue certain traits because, for whatever reason, we come to think of them as important. In one study, people from the Midwest and California thought that Californians were happier because—hey, sunshine, the beach—but both groups measure up the same in happiness, in part because people underestimate the influence of the pleasantness of day-to-day life (the Midwest has a lot of it) and overestimate how much sunshine really makes you happy (it's there all the time so you take it for granted).[10]

So when it comes to the class versus race issue around admissions, a plausible explanation for why people overestimate Black wealth and, hence, overlook the continued need for race-conscious admissions is that people easily get anchored into believing some piece of information, such as the image of Malia Obama's existence, or incomplete, misleadingly presented data, such as the idea that 86 percent of Black families at elite institutions are middle or upper income. Never mind that Black students far outpace White students among low- and middle-income students and that White students are three times more likely to come from upper-income families. These lines of thinking become "anchors" in people's minds, serving as filters through which they process other evidence.

In a column for the Institute for Policy Studies, attorney Antonio Moore suggests that people severely underestimate the Black-White wealth disparity because the prominent presence of Black celebrities in the NBA, NFL, and entertainment industry have, for many, become mental anchors for the state of African American wealth and economic stability.[11] However, in reality, Black celebrities make up a miniscule percentage of the overall African American population. Moore explains that African Americans are severely underrepresented among the country's wealthiest, being only 1 percent of the S&P 500 CEOs. To top it off, White families own *98 percent of the land in the United States*, and African American home ownership is lower now than it was in the Great Depression of the 1930s. Moore comments that "wealth in America is simply not diverse, and that reality remains true no matter how many times we are shown LeBron James in his mansion in feel-good commercials."[12] LeBron, Malia Obama, and others (*The Cosby Show* anyone?) are powerful anchors. Ironically, while many people overestimate Black wealth, they also overestimate the rate of crimes committed by Blacks. A study led by Justin Pickett at the University of Albany found that Whites overestimated the rate of violent crimes committed by African Americans by more than 2 to 1.[13] Clearly, something is messed up about the public's general anchors for how we think about Black America.

So that's a stab at what's going on in people's minds. Now let's get back to the data.

THE DATA SAY WE NEED RACE TO GET TO CLASS—REALLY

The assessment of social class itself without the context of race/ethnicity is incomplete. Indeed, considering race is necessary to assessing the full-extent of socioeconomic disadvantage, which is ironic since Kahlenberg,

Edward Blum (the guy behind both of the University of Texas, Austin, Supreme Court affirmative action lawsuits), and others claim that affirmative action based on class alone is the only way to help the "truly disadvantaged." The role of race in properly assessing socioeconomic disadvantage is backed up by recent cutting-edge statistical analyses led by Sean Reardon and colleagues which shows that colleges and universities get the most socioeconomic diversity by giving strong consideration to both race *and* social class.[14] In other words, all other things held constant, an admissions model that weighs race/ethnicity and social class as favorable attributes results in more low-income students than a model that ignores race but still gives a strong preference based on social class. Are you tracking with me here? The best way to get to more low-income students in higher education is not to ditch race but to strongly consider both race and class. Even for a researcher like me, who has seen time again that race-neutral models do not produce sufficient racial diversity, to see that race-conscious models can get more *socioeconomic* diversity than class-based affirmative action is surprising. Nerd moment: This is the beauty of data upturning our preconceived notions.

Let's dig into the data. Reardon and colleagues reviewed admissions data for forty colleges and universities to simulate what kind of admissions and enrollment outcomes would come from a variety of scenarios; they even combined various levels of preferences related to race/ethnicity with different levels of class-based preferences. So, at one end of the spectrum is a simulation of giving no weight at all to race or social class, and at the other end is a simulation that gives strong preference to both. In the middle are different combinations of these scenarios—for example, giving no weight to race but moderate weight to class or giving moderate weight to race and moderate weight to class.[15]

The study improves on previous simulations of admissions in a variety of ways. First, the sample includes forty colleges, which is way more than high-profile studies like Espenshade and Radford's or Matthew Gaertner's simulation of admissions at the University of Colorado.[16] (Interestingly, class-based affirmative action proponents love drawing on Gaertner's very interesting work to argue that racial diversity can be achieved without race-conscious admissions. But why are we trying to make national policy decisions for the country's highly selective universities based on a simulation from a university that has an 80 percent acceptance rate?) Okay, back to Reardon and colleagues. They use a fancy method called agent-based simulation, which takes into account all the quirks in trying to estimate the decision-making processes of high school seniors and colleges. Trust me, it's good stuff.

In their analysis, they divide students into five quintiles based on socioeconomic status, where Q1 represents students from the lowest quintile and Q5 is the highest. I'll classify Q1 and Q2 as representing students from a low-income background. The simulation that produces the highest percentage of low-income representation came from the model that gave a strong preference based on both race and class, resulting in 23 percent lower-income students from Q1 and Q2 combined.[17] It surpasses the model that gives no bump to race/ethnicity but gives a strong preference to social class (21.6 percent low-income students). These numbers, 23 percent versus 21.6 percent, may not seem too different, but the "strong race, strong class" model results in a notably higher representation of students from the lowest socioeconomic quintile (Q1): 16 percent versus 7.6 percent. In other words, a race-conscious model that also gives strong weight to social class results in *more than twice as many* of the lowest-income students enrolling.

It's worth a detour to discuss how strong or moderate preference was defined in the study. After all, some folks may not be comfortable with the idea of a "strong" preference related to race. However, never fear, it's not much more than what's already being done. According to Reardon and colleagues, "Strong racial affirmative action is slightly stronger than the average used by highly selective colleges today; moderate racial affirmative action is half as strong."[18] For class-based preference, "strong" is equated with two to four times the preference currently used by selective colleges. So for this scenario to work, colleges would need to be more assertive around social class, as they should be. But it is compelling to note that maximizing socioeconomic diversity requires attention given to race—and not much more than what is already given, wherein colleges give some consideration to race/ethnicity in combination with numerous other traits demonstrating excellence.

Although Reardon and colleagues' model isn't perfect, it helps us understand how the socioeconomic composition of institutions would vary in different scenarios when other factors are held constant—a valuable service. While giving moderate preference to both race/ethnicity and social class results in only 16.5 percent representation from the lower two quintiles, that scenario exceeds the one where no consideration is given to race/ethnicity and moderate preference is given to social class (13.3 percent).[19] Consistently, considering race/ethnicity *in combination with* social class bolsters socioeconomic diversity.

What do these scenarios mean for racial/ethnic diversity? Not only does a scenario giving strong preference to both race/ethnicity and social class result in the most socioeconomic diversity, it also results in the most racial/ethnic diversity, a predicted 43.1 percent representation of students of color.[20] The next highest representation, at 24.7 percent, comes from institutions that give moderate preference to both. The number drops even further, to 17.6 percent, for a scenario that gives strong preference to social class but no consideration to race. This isn't that far from the percentage of students of color, 14.4 percent, if no consideration at all were given to race or social class. It's notable that giving strong preference to social class but *no* consideration to race only results in a 3.2 percentage point increase in students of color over the model that completely ignores social class. As Reardon and colleagues summarize, "Kahlenberg (1996) has argued that 'class-based preferences provide a constitutional way to achieve greater racial and ethnic diversity.' Yet, based on our simulations, SES-based affirmative action policies do not seem likely to be effective at producing racial diversity."[21]

The complexities of these race-based and SES-based findings challenge the assertion that class-based affirmative action would directly boost racial/ethnic diversity, as claimed by Kahlenberg and other proponents. Not only is the percent of students of color higher under scenarios that give moderate or strong consideration to race, the percentage of students of color under a "strong class no race scenario" barely exceeds the number who would attend selective colleges if these schools wholly ignored class and race altogether. In other words, even strong consideration of social class does not appear to have much of an additive effect for racial diversity.

It's not that the world is neatly divided into advantaged versus disadvantaged students of color, and that you can seamlessly ensure that you're admitting all the disadvantaged ones by ignoring race and considering only class. Socioeconomic diversity increases when you weigh not just class alone but class *and* race. The same goes for racial diversity, where we see the most racial diversity in scenarios that consider both race *and* class strongly. Older analyses suggest that part of the reason why class-based affirmative action is ineffective for boosting racial diversity is because low-income White students outnumber low-income students of color, even if a higher percentage of URM students identify as low-income.[22] While this pattern still holds, newer analyses suggest that class-based affirmative action is also limited in boosting socioeconomic diversity because class-alone preferences fail to capture the full extent of socioeconomic disadvantage within communities of color.

ADDRESSING UNDERMATCH: AN IMPORTANT, BUT NOT A FIX-ALL, SOLUTION

Another deterrent to equity in higher education is the issue of undermatch, the phenomenon of students, disproportionately from low-income backgrounds, attending less selective institutions than they are potentially qualified for. With undermatching, a talent pool eligible to attend more selective and prestigious institutions misses out on that opportunity. And because selective institutions tend to be feeders to elite graduate programs and careers, these students are possibly missing out on a chance for accelerated social mobility. So, a student might attend Towson College when they would be competitive at the University of Maryland, College Park, or a valedictorian of a rural high school ends up at a lower-ranked commuter institution when they might be Ivy League material. By estimates, as many as 25,000 to 35,000 high school seniors are undermatched each year.[23]

This trend presents a real challenge. Low-income students have much to bring to more selective institutions. In turn, they could benefit from those institutions' resources, such as small class sizes and the abundance of cocurricular opportunities. However, class-based affirmative action advocates have presented fixing undermatch as being best remedied by class-based affirmative action, posing race-conscious admissions strategies and addressing undermatch as either-or propositions. In their spin on the issues, persistent racial inequality is more a thing of the past, and undermatch is a reflection of the current problem of class inequality. Hence, they view race-conscious admissions as an outdated strategy for addressing the "real" problem of undermatch, which they view as a class-based phenomenon.[24] To the class-based affirmative action advocates who push for solutions to undermatch, there is a ready pool of talented, low-income students ready to attend elite institutions—and part of the problem is that their spaces are being filled with ostensibly less-qualified students who are admitted via race-conscious admissions policies.

There are two problems with this way of thinking. First, addressing undermatching is more complicated than it looks. According to those who lobby that eradicating race is the key to solving undermatch, if you didn't admit all those URM students who benefit from race-conscious admissions, you'd have more room to admit the low-income kids who have higher SAT scores but currently attend less selective colleges. Yet admissions is much more complicated than a formulaic process of simplistic matchmaking where you have certain low-income students with a certain SAT score, and if you just admitted them they would come and everyone would be happy.

Michael Bastedo of the University of Michigan has done some of the most thoughtful writing on undermatch, highlighting other factors for why it's not actually so predictable where a student, even one with a good SAT score, may land for college. In particular, he notes that the nature of holistic admissions and selective admissions means that a strong SAT score does not guarantee admission to the country's top colleges. Bastedo and colleague Allyson Flaster note that "given this complexity, undermatching researchers are simply overconfident in their ability to predict who has access to selective colleges."[25] These complex processes are not a reason to ignore undermatch altogether; undermatch is a more complicated phenomena than simply the formula of "Well, if we got rid of race in admissions, these students would get swept up into more selective colleges and the world would be all better."[26] For Bastedo and Flaster, claims that "fixing" undermatch is the golden ticket to eradicating class-based inequality are overstated:

> Yet research that examines the evolution of institutional stratification suggests that adhering more strongly to an education based meritocracy in college admissions does not reduce gaps in college access between advantaged and disadvantaged students . . . High-income students benefit disproportionately in the competition for academic achievement throughout their lives. The tournament system of mobility practiced in the United States allows ample time for class-based disparities in financial and social capital to influence the distribution of "merit" that matters for college admission, and thus for eventual placement in the occupational hierarchy. As a result, even if students were "perfectly matched" to institutions, low-income students would not benefit systematically.[27]

To echo their words: it's not that undermatch isn't a problem worth addressing, it's just that even if we fix it, we're not going to wipe away all class inequality in education. Undermatch has gained traction because it's an easy, tangible issue to understand (or think you understand), and some folks have proposed a "simple," tangible solution: just ban race in admissions. In chapter 5 we'll learn more about a term called *bikeshedding*, a phenomena that explains why our brains latch on to simple solutions that inadequately address the big problem. Unfortunately, class inequality extends way beyond undermatch, and critically addressing it remains a worthy endeavor.

Pitting undermatch against race-conscious approaches as mutually exclusive options does everyone a disservice because race-conscious approaches are part of the solution to reducing undermatch. The racial wealth gap indicates that systemic inequality is not solely a class-based issue; it operates along both racial and economic lines. Giving strong consideration to both race and class would likely result in student bodies that are not just more racially diverse, but more socioeconomically diverse, as shown by Reardon and colleagues. Undermatch is not going to be solved from one broad-brushed policy solution of eliminating race-conscious admissions altogether; rather, it's going to take conscious targeting of local populations. This means that admissions officers need all the information they can get—including, but not limited to, race/ethnicity—to understand the full context of where a student is coming from. The operation of race-conscious admissions, which does not exclude the consideration of social class, utilizes approaches that are highly institution specific and contextual. In other words, what works at the University of Colorado will not work at Harvard. UCLA has different needs than the University of Oregon. And likewise, addressing undermatch is going to involve careful attention to local context and institutional dynamics.

Reducing undermatch is an important goal for higher education, but it is not an either-or trade-off that the class-based affirmative action proponents would like you to believe. It is a complex combination of widening the applicant pool so that the most talented students apply, attend, and persist. It requires addressing financial aid and, yes, giving greater consideration to the multiple dimensions of social class. And none of these things preclude the additional consideration of race/ethnicity during the admissions process, which is a necessary tool to maximize both socioeconomic and racial diversity and address the persistent inequality in our country.

SOCIOECONOMIC DIVERSITY AND THE CAMPUS RACIAL CLIMATE—ADDRESSING BOTH RACE AND CLASS

Just as we need to consider race to get to more economic diversity, sometimes we need to pay attention to social class to support a positive racial climate. Socioeconomic diversity exists within racial/ethnic groups and can promote "relative equal status" between students, one of the conditions needed for healthy intergroup interaction, as established by pioneering social scientist Gordon Allport.[28] The assumption for too long has been that students of different races share relative equal status because they are all, well, students. However, this approach misses the inequalities linked to both race and class that permeate students' lives both prior to and during college. Students do not leave that structural inequality behind when they enter college; the perniciousness of racial stereotypes and economic disparities do not magically disappear on enrollment. Students of color often encounter a campus climate that is isolating and unfriendly to them, where there are frequent reminders and symbols of that inequality—everything from an offensive "ghetto"-themed party being thrown by a White fraternity to the feeling that comes from being the only woman of color in a large lecture hall. Perhaps not paying attention to the nuances behind relative equal status is one reason colleges continually struggle with how to get students to interact with each other across racial/ethnic lines.

Fostering socioeconomic diversity within racial/ethnic groups can help bridge some of the inequality that exists between majority- and minority-status groups. A certain amount of social distance (inequality) usually exists between White and URM students; however, this gap can be widened when, for instance, White students disproportionately come from upper-class backgrounds and URM students come almost solely from lower-income backgrounds. Class inequality is layered on racial inequality, strengthening existing racial/ethnic boundaries. However, if there is greater socioeconomic diversity within each racial/ethnic group, racial inequality does not totally disappear, but there is less opportunity for balkanization to exist along both racial *and* economic lines, as there are low-income, middle-income, and upper-income Whites and their URM counterparts. Low-income Whites may serve as a bridge between the two groups, just as middle-income URM students may find commonality with peers of other races who share an economic background.

Interacting across race in a society that is deeply segregated by race is taxing. It's simply easier to be with your own kind, which is why the status quo of human relations is something called *homophily*—birds of a feather flock together. On a college campus, social distance and inequality don't just exist along racial lines (Black versus White) or along economic lines (rich versus low income) but along identities that are intersectional: there is more social distance between, say, a low-income URM student and a rich White student than there is between a middle-income URM student and a middle-income White student. Don't get me wrong—in a society characterized by racial inequality, where, yes, walking around campus as a Black male could get you questioned by the police with potentially disastrous or even life-threatening results, there is still categorical inequality that exists between middle-income URM students and their middle-income White peers. But there is arguably even more social distance to bridge when vast economic inequality is layered on already existing racial inequality.

When we have students of different racial/ethnic groups of diverse socioeconomic backgrounds, we have a more fluid, porous environment for interracial interaction.[29] Instead of having balkanization that is based on the intertwined forces of race *and* class, we have greater fluidity when we have students of different socioeconomic backgrounds who can help bridge the gap between various racial/ethnic groups. Think of how it's easier to interact with someone who's different in one respect (say, race/ethnicity) when they share something in common with you—maybe religion, a passion for science, or knowledge of what it's like to grow up in a rural community. These commonalities are critical to help build bridges between students of different race/ethnicities, and socioeconomic background can be one of these traits. So instead of a campus where you have majority status (White and East Asian American students) coming from almost all higher-income backgrounds and URM students coming from almost all lower-income backgrounds—a scenario where there is much social distance to be bridged across race—you have White, East Asian, Black, Latinx, you-name-it students of diverse socioeconomic backgrounds. This is what sets the stage for a more fluid environment for interracial interaction because there are more opportunities for bridging social distance and enhancing opportunities for relative equal status among students.

So yes, we need to pay more attention to social class, but in combination with race. In an article in the *American Educational Research Journal*, Nida Denson, Nicholas Bowman, and I found that socioeconomic diversity on its own neither subsumes nor replaces the positive effects linked with having racial diversity in the student body when it comes to triggering the educational benefits of diversity.[30] Racial diversity in a student body is irreplaceable, and race-conscious policies are needed to help make that happen. But attention to socioeconomic status in combination with racial diversity can hopefully create a more fluid environment for interracial interaction, benefiting students across the spectrum.

WRAPPING IT UP ON RECOGNIZING BOTH RACE AND CLASS IN ADMISSIONS

By now you probably know more about the perils of solely relying on class-based affirmative action than you ever wanted to know. To recap, addressing race and addressing class is not an either-or proposition. Campuses are best served by admissions policies that help them understand a student's context for educational opportunity and potential to contribute to the diversity of the student body, and this means considering both race and class in admissions. In fact, policies that give strong consideration to both race *and* class would likely result in greater socioeconomic diversity than policies that only address social class. All of this is because of the unique ways that inequality cuts across not just economic lines but racial *and* economic lines.

Don't believe the falsehood that the Black middle class and the White middle class are on equal terms. Wealth for the median White family exceeds wealth for the median Black family by 15 to 1.[31] Yes, that's fifteen times more wealth! So while the Obamas may be doing pretty well, the existence of some affluent Black families does not negate the reality that the wealth gap in America is still deeply racialized. And both low- and middle-income African American families would still benefit deeply from race-conscious admissions policies, because the persistent negative conditions affect schooling and life opportunities for even middle-class Black families.[32]

The need to address both race and class goes beyond admission to an institution, however; it affects race relations once students arrive on campus. To maximize interracial engagement (and, more specifically, to strengthen relative equal status between students), we need considerable socioeconomic diversity within racial/ethnic groups.[33] We want to challenge the consolidation of privilege that occurs when universities are dominated not just by White students but White wealthy students, leading to campus spaces that are balkanized not just by race but by race and class. Extending race-conscious admissions to include middle-income URM students is also vital to boost the critical mass of students of color needed to challenge the isolation that occurs all too easily due to limited representation of a particular racial/ethnic group. Remember: being middle class and Black can look really different from being middle class and White due to the racial wealth gap. Boosting critical mass by fostering socioeconomic diversity within racial/ethnic groups is also critical to challenge stereotypes that link race and class (e.g., the assumption that *all* URM students are from poor backgrounds).

And while we do need to pay greater attention to social class in admissions, it should not, and need not, come at the expense of knowing a student's race. Excluding the consideration of race could have serious negative consequences for campus diversity and the racial/socioeconomic composition of the student body. So, don't believe the false choice that you have to pick only one. The Supreme Court has affirmed repeatedly a system that is holistic and considers both, as well as an array of other factors and traits. There is no formula that guarantees admissions for anyone; admissions officers need as much information as they can get to make decisions. And don't believe the lie that economic inequality is only remedied through race-neutral policies. The tentacles of inequality are, unfortunately, much more complex than that, and we need policies and practitioners that adequately address that complexity.

CHAPTER FOUR

Why Affirmative Action Is Good for Asian Americans

ON AUGUST 1, 2017, America woke up to the news that the US Department of Justice was planning to investigate whether colleges and universities were discriminating against White students through their affirmative action policies.[1] A chill went through educators and policy makers nationwide. The same heavy-handedness that had imposed a sweeping travel ban, threatened to drastically limit immigration, and sought to ban transgender people from the military was now ready to make a hit on education policy. Despite the Supreme Court affirming race-conscious admissions policies twice in recent years, eliminating affirmative action was still on the conservative agenda.*

*I served as a consulting expert for The President and Fellows of Harvard College (Harvard Corporation) ("Harvard") in connection with the matter of *Students for Fair Admissions, Inc. v. Harvard*, Civ. Act. No. 1:14-14176. The views and opinions expressed here are my own and do not reflect Harvard's views or information learned from Harvard in the course of my consulting work.

A later statement from the Department of Justice clarified that the Trump administration was recruiting attorneys to work on a specific strand of the affirmative action debate. According to spokeswoman Sarah Isgur Flores, "The posting sought volunteers to investigate one administrative complaint filed by a coalition of 64 Asian American associations in May 2015 that the prior Administration left unresolved . . . The complaint alleges racial discrimination against Asian Americans in a university's admissions policy and practices."[2]

Asian Americans? For years, the strategy to challenge affirmative action in the courts was to recruit a White female plaintiff who had somewhat mediocre or above-average-but-not-stellar academic credentials and then sue some university. After noticing that it didn't work in *Grutter*, *Fisher I*, or *Fisher II*, Edward Blum, the mastermind behind both *Fisher* cases who also tried to dismantle the Voting Rights Act in his spare time, decided to change tactics. He set up a website featuring an Asian American student staring pensively into the distance, accompanied by the headline "Were You Rejected by Harvard? It May Be Because You're the Wrong Race."[3] In case that message was too subtle, the insignia on the website's top left corner blared: "HARVARD UNIVERSITY: NOT FAIR."

My only surprise is that it took the anti–affirmative action movement decades to realize that Asian Americans with SATs of 1500-plus, stellar GPAs, and many quality extracurricular activities (They read to the elderly! They fund-raise for NPR! They train drug-sniffing dogs!) make for a stronger challenge to race-conscious admissions policies than White folks with B averages. (When they say that Asian Americans are "invisible" in American society, they really mean it.) You know it was bad when Twitter erupted with the hashtag #beckywiththebadgrades to celebrate after the Supreme Court ruled against Abigail Fisher for the second time in *Fisher II*. Not super nice, but they had a point.

#beckywiththegoodgrades, aka the Asian Americans that Ed Blum and company recruited to sue Harvard through the lawsuit *Students for Fair Admissions v. Harvard*, might make a more sympathetic plaintiff than

Abigail Fisher, but the deeper problem remains—just because students have great grades, test scores, accomplishments, and experiences doesn't mean that anyone is guaranteed admission into Harvard or any other highly selective institution.

The anti–affirmative action movement would have you believe that this is because Asian Americans are penalized by race-conscious admissions policies, disadvantaged by affirmative action, and rampantly and intentionally discriminated against in the selective college admissions process. It's a compelling and heartbreaking story. The problem is that it's misleading and wrong.

In this chapter I address the prevailing myth that Asian American kids are systematically discriminated against in college admissions and that the way to prevent this is to get rid of race-conscious affirmative action. I also address the related myths that Asian Americans are uniformly disadvantaged by any system that considers race and that they would be best served by a system that eliminates the consideration of race/ethnicity. Finally, I talk about ways that race-conscious admissions actually works to the benefit of Asian Americans, universities, and society. To note, some of the issues I'll reference—the Harvard lawsuit and other ongoing litigation—are pending as I write, and who knows what the state of affirmative action will be by the time you read this book. Regardless of what happens with the courts, this chapter will help you understand the issues in a more complex and nuanced way.

THE ANTI–AFFIRMATIVE ACTION MOVEMENT: FACTS OR FEAR-MONGERING?

Proposition 209, the 1996 ordinance that banned race-conscious admissions in California, has been devastating to the enrollment of URM students at many of the highly regarded University of California campuses. At Berkeley, African American enrollment was at just 2.5 percent in the fall of 2016.[4] In comparison, thanks to aggressive outreach, UCLA is somewhat higher after record lows for many years, to 4.8 percent in the fall of 2016. That percentage might not seem that great, but in 2006 there were only one hundred African American freshmen. One hundred out of 4,811 first-year students![5] The slight growth in UCLA's numbers conceals continuing inequities: a disproportionately high percentage (65 percent) of Black male undergraduates are athletes, and Black males make up a very slim portion (1.9 percent) of the overall male enrollment.[6] Similarly, UC San Diego can boast that African American enrollment has risen 150 percent in the last ten years, from 1 percent in 2006 to a whopping 2 percent in 2016.[7] Yikes. Why are these numbers so low when *half* of California public school graduates are either African American or Latinx?[8] To make things worse, Prop 209 has created a negative cycle wherein some suspect that the Black students who actually are accepted to UC institutions are increasingly turning down offers due to the negative racial climate of various campuses.[9]

This all had the opportunity to change. In 2012 Senate Constitutional Amendment 5 (SCA-5) was introduced, which proposed allowing, but not requiring, consideration of race/ethnicity in California's public higher education for admissions, recruitment, and retention initiatives. It didn't mean admitting on the basis of race/ethnicity (illegal) but simply allowing admissions officers to know a student's race/ethnicity and take it into account in understanding the profile of a student. A grassroots campaign opposing SCA-5 erupted in 2014, and, to the surprise of many, it was spearheaded by subsets of the Asian American community—in particular, more recent immigrants from mainland China. Heavy pressure was put on Asian American legislators who had already signed on to SCA-5 to withdraw their support for the amendment. Eventually, several Asian American legislators got the vote indefinitely tabled, and SCA-5 was seen as dead in the water.

Arguably, the anti-SCA-5 campaign was rooted in fearmongering and misinformation about what bringing race-conscious admissions would mean for Asian Americans in particular. Words like "quotas," "bans," and "ceilings" on Asian American enrollment—all of which are illegal, by the way—were used in articles circulated online and in the ethnic media, preying on many people's fear that the system was somehow stacked against them. One letter written by a child to his local congressman that went viral summed up the fears well: "Dear Congressman Maienschein. My name is [deleted]. I am 8 years old . . . I want to be able to go to college in California when I grow up. Please help stop SCA-5. I don't think it's fair if I can't go to college in California just because I'm Asian American. Sincerely, [name deleted]."[10]

Where did this confusion and misinformation come from? Part of it likely stems from misunderstandings of how selective admissions works in the United States and in the UC system. Here, universities perform a holistic review of an applicant in the local context of the educational opportunities provided to them and consider numerous criteria, such as essays, extracurricular achievements, demonstrated leadership or grit, teacher recommendations, and the like. In Asia, though, college admissions is generally determined by a single test score, a practice that reflects the belief that SAT scores (the presumed equivalent of the "big test" in Asian countries) reign supreme. In turn, an extensive test prep industry has sprung up in areas with high concentrations of Asian Americans.[11] So I can understand why the idea of reintroducing race into the UC admissions system was worrisome to some Asian Americans, particularly those who more recently came from East Asia, where no equivalent system exists.[12] More recent immigrants may also be less familiar with the history of inequality and disenfranchisement that continues to affect educational opportunity for URM students in California.

Race-conscious admissions has nothing to do with quotas or ceilings on any racial/ethnic group; such measures are explicitly illegal and have been since the *Bakke* Supreme Court decision in 1978. Yet, to someone from another country, one where the culture is so heavily constructed around a single make-or-break test score, hearing that race/ethnicity could have any sort of role in college admissions would be alarming.

140 POINTS: RESEARCH TAKEN OUT OF CONTEXT

Another big factor in the SCA-5 drama was how research by Thomas Espenshade, Alexandria Walton Radford, and associates went viral. In 2009, Espenshade and Radford published their study of eight institutions, the National Study of College Experience, in the book *No Longer Separate, Not Yet Equal: Race and Class in Elite College Admission and Campus Life*. In a chapter provocatively titled "What Counts in Being Admitted?" the part that went viral was a finding that Asian Americans supposedly had to outscore Whites by 140 on the SAT to be admitted to a selective private college or university and that African American students had the equivalent of a 310 point boost and Latinx students a 130 point boost in comparison to White students.[13] The authors also found that, all other things held equal, in 1997, 1 in 5 Asian Americans was accepted into the sample institutions, versus 1 in 3 for other racial/ethnic groups.[14] The "140 points" statistic went viral. And, as you can imagine, some Asians were not happy to hear this.

I can understand the outrage. A standardized test presumes fairness or equity: everyone has the same chance to study for and take the test. (Or do they? I'll discuss this later.) It gets measured and evaluated the same no matter who takes it, thanks to ScanTron. So wouldn't it be blatantly unfair if Asian Americans were being docked 140 or however many points on the SAT—those hard-won points earned through late nights of studying and trudging to prep classes in the summer—just to compete at the same levels as Whites?

The problem is that Espenshade and Radford's study has been interpreted in ways that reach beyond the limits of what the actual study is able to say because of its sample and design; accordingly, the authors note that their findings are not proof that colleges are discriminating against Asian Americans. All research studies have limitations, ways they are not able to account for every single relevant factor. There are also limitations to how much findings can speak to actual conclusions or recommendations for policy. With their numbers and confusing statistical methods, research studies can easily have the air of authoritative impenetrability, but it is far too easy for people to jump to conclusions that don't actually match what the data are able to speak to. In these cases, readers may overgeneralize the findings of a study beyond the researchers' original intent.

The Espenshade and Radford study examines the probability of admission using students from eight institutions, a decent spread but not necessarily representative of all selective institutions.[15] The authors took into account things like a student's class rank, GPA, SAT score, and number of Advanced Placement tests taken. However, admissions officers use a broader slate of factors that Espenshade and Radford did not include in their analysis, such as essays, teacher recommendations, extracurricular activities, leadership experiences, potential for leadership, and high school quality. When it comes to extracurricular activities, it's not just counting the number of leadership positions held; it's looking with a nuanced eye at the *quality* of experiences, what *meaning* a student is able to derive from the experience, and the like. It's weighing how to evaluate a low-income candidate who didn't have time to play varsity sports but spent twenty-five hours per week bagging groceries while helping take care of a sick relative. It's reading between the lines to decide if a student is trying to check off the boxes by doing community service or is the type of person who is will make it a lifelong commitment. It's also evaluating the opportunities a student had to engage in their activities or accomplishments—does it mean more when a student did some of these things when they weren't allowed to take the school's textbooks home versus a student whose compelling service trip to South America was bankrolled by their parents?

My point in all of this (other than acquainting you with how incredibly hard an admissions officer's job can be) is to show all of the stuff that Espenshade and Radford's analyses weren't able to account for. But if you don't trust me, take it from the man himself. When interviewed about the subject, Espenshade stated, "I understand the worry of Asian students, but do I have a smoking gun? No."[16] In another interview, he said: "This doesn't mean there is discrimination [against Asian Americans]. We don't have access to all the information an admissions dean does. We don't have extracurriculars. We don't have personal statements or guidance counselors' recommendations. We're missing some stuff."[17]

So, does this mean that Asian Americans in some way have worse nonstandardized accomplishments and achievements than non–Asian Americans?[18] Not necessarily, but other factors may be at play. As a former admissions reader who spent many years reviewing applications to the UC system, Oiyan Poon, a professor at Colorado State University, "often noticed patterns in the ways many applicants presented their essay narratives. For example, I commonly read essays by Asian American applicants about their families' immigration experiences that celebrated how their parents or grandparents overcame adversities but did not focus on the student's personal experiences and accomplishments. As a result, such essays did not present information about the student that I, as an evaluator, could score."[19]

As Espenshade himself said, his data is no smoking gun, and nuances in how Asian American students talk about their own experiences might account for some of the discrepancies. What we *can* say from Espenshade's data is that when you don't account for nonstandardized metrics, Asian Americans admitted to institutions in the dataset have SAT scores that are significantly higher than their White, Black, and Latinx counterparts. But that doesn't necessarily mean that Asian Americans *need* higher SAT scores to get into particular institutions. They *have* them, yes, but having and needing are two different things.

Asian Americans have higher SAT scores likely because participation in SAT preparation is exceptionally high among East Asian American subpopulations, a trend that cuts across social class for certain subgroups. In a study I did of college students, 46.7 percent of low-income Korean Americans took a SAT preparation class, as compared to 42 percent of their rich White peers.[20] Take a second to absorb that—I'll discuss it in the next chapter on SAT prep.

Regarding SAT prep, there's a lot of it going on in East Asian American communities. Part of this is in response to the idea that Asian Americans *need* higher SAT scores (versus *having* higher SAT scores, on average), which creates a vicious cycle where everyone is studying harder because of the self-perceived *need* to keep up with the Joneses (or the Changs).[21] The forces behind this pattern are complicated, but many Asian Americans exist in a world where there is heavy socialization around the importance of standardized testing. It's a unique combination of having connections to Asia, where everything rises and falls on a single test, the availability of test prep options due to the ethnic economy, immigration patterns, and the complicated set of expectations that have come to be associated with being Asian American.[22] Sociologists Jennifer Lee and Min Zhou refer to the latter as the "success frame," a set of cognitive frames that influence what Asian Americans, and East Asian Americans in particular, have come to see as normal and expected behavior.[23] There is no mystical Asian value around education.[24] Rather, a complicated set of norms and expectations connect to waves of immigration, the communities built by immigrants, and the external pressures of a racialized and, arguably, racist society.[25] The wave that "set the pace" for much of this was a subset of post-1965 Asian immigrants who were highly educated, *not* a random sampling of the Asian population. You can imagine that these post-1965 cohorts had high expectations for their kids, which was probably more of a by-product of social class than some innate, mysterious formula for Asian success. However, as explained by Lee and Zhou, over time these expectations became linked with race/ethnicity, creating a set of expectations and norms internalized by many Asian Americans—even if they may not live up to them.[26] After all, 40 percent of Asian Americans attend not Harvard but community colleges.[27] Additionally, these expectations were reinforced by society through the rampant stereotyping of Asian Americans as being academically successful—a.k.a., the model minority myth, which also works to denigrate other minority groups ("Why can't you be successful like Asian Americans?").[28]

So yes, Asian Americans *have* higher test scores. Do they *need* them? Yes and no. Everyone needs some sort of decently high score to signal to colleges that "I'm pretty good" (as in, "I can take a test and do pretty well at it because, hey, college has a lot of tests"). But does any test score guarantee admission to an elite institution? Absolutely not. The false rhetoric around Asian Americans needing a certain test score to get into an institution promotes the misconception that there are basically minimum cut-off scores for each racial/ethnic group and that the score for Asian Americans is higher. This idea is patently and deeply false. Again, remember that Espenshade and Radford dispute claims that their research is bulletproof evidence that discrimination exists against Asian Americans in the college admissions process. In their book they note plain and simple: "With the information at hand, however, we are not able to settle the question of whether Asian applicants experience discrimination in elite college admissions."[29]

COGNITIVE BIASES AND WHY "140 POINTS" WENT VIRAL

An interlude to consider what research can tell us about why the rumor of Asian Americans experiencing discrimination in admissions took off, to the point of "140 points" becoming a widely spread piece of misinformation—how and why did this soundbite go viral? I've walked you through the reasoning behind why the idea is misleading. Blah blah statistics blah blah interpretations don't match the data or research design blah blah. All of that is true and good; but to be honest, most people don't pay close attention to the alignment between research design and subsequent interpretations. What they do pay attention to are nuggets of information that match their existing suspicions about how the world works—*confirmation bias*, which is a widespread form of cognitive bias.

Unpacking confirmation bias can help us think about why the "140 points" bit took off. There are some decent reasons why, even prior to

Espenshade and Radford, folks in the Asian American community wondered if there might be some form of discrimination against them in admissions. Even those who recognize the diversity of the community are not immune to internalizing the model minority stereotype: there are all of these so-called Asian Whiz Kids, yet some of them are getting rejected from top schools—something must be wrong! Not to mention that there actually were documented cases of this happening in the 1980s, when there actually *were* ceilings and caps put on Asian American applicants at UCLA. Even though these cases were condemned and the corresponding federal investigation sent a loud message that these policies were unacceptable, people still wonder, Is it happening? And last, there is some level of suspicion among many Asian Americans that they do have to work harder than White folks to reach the same level of accomplishment, or that their accomplishments are not always rewarded in the same ways that White people's are. Besides the existence of the bamboo ceiling or general stereotypes of Asian Americans as not being leadership material, this last one actually has some backing in the data, and not just for the well-educated. Sociologists ChangHwan Kim and Arthur Sakamoto found that even less-educated Asian American men earn less than their White peers with the same levels of education.[30]

So put all of that together and what do you have but chunks of the community that are pretty receptive to ideas around Asian Americans being discriminated against in admissions. Hence, fertile ground for the occurrence of confirmation bias when the Espenshade and Radford study came out. Even though Espenshade himself said that the data were not evidence of discrimination, many assumed it was. The data and their aura of authority as "research" were enough to confirm the hunches that some folks already had about the admissions system being stacked against them. Really, the surprising and amazing thing is that so many Asian Americans support affirmative action to begin with—generally at least 50 percent in national polls and as high as in the 60–70 percent range in iterations of the National Asian American Survey.[31] So the assumption that Asian Americans uniformly disagree with policies like affirmative action, which were founded to advance racial justice, are unfounded. The *data* tell us a different story about who Asian Americans are and what they support.

Alright, so that's how confirmation bias works. So how do ideas, and in some cases faulty ideas, spread? A helpful concept is the *availability cascade*, coined by Timur Kuran of Duke University and Cass Sunstein of Harvard. As explained in their paper published in the *Stanford Law Review*: "An availability cascade is a self-reinforcing process of collective belief formation by which an expressed perception triggers a chain reaction that gives the perception of increasing plausibility through its rising availability in public discourse."[32] Kuran and Sunstein describe this process as mediated by the availability heuristic, where "the probability assessments we make as individuals are frequently based on the ease with which we can think of relevant examples."[33] In short, the accumulation of a critical mass of people who come to see a particular belief as memorable and feasible due to the availability heuristic triggers an availability cascade, wherein certain ideas seem more likely or possible due to their increasing visibility (or "availability"). You can think of it as a fancy version of mental peer pressure, or groupthink (another cognitive bias), but with more specificity around how the different mechanisms are triggered. While Kuran and Sunstein discuss the availability cascade largely in the context of financial risk and regulation, they point out that it is helpful for explaining things like the rise and fall of McCarthyism, various social movements, and, yes, the rise and subsequent public opposition to affirmative action.[34]

In the case of the spread of the "140 points" hysteria, Espenshade and Radford's research (or rather, research misinterpreted and taken out of statistical context) was seen as evidence of some preexisting hunches that Asian Americans were getting the short end of the stick, which already existed within parts of the Asian American community. For people unfamiliar with the selective university system of holistic admissions, the idea that any group needs a higher SAT score would naturally seem inappropriate—a grave injustice. "140 points" is a short, snappy soundbite that easily lent itself to being repeated in community networks, ethnic news outlets, and social media. A prime example of the availability heuristic, where something easy to recall becomes seen as not just possible but true.

Additionally, when the SCA-5 debacle exploded, there were other recent developments that promoted the idea of discrimination against Asian Americans in admissions. A big one was Ron Unz's 2012 article in the *American Conservative* claiming there were anti-Asian quotas in the Ivy League (and, of course, it included the 140 points tidbit).[35] Unz spent a lot of the piece making the case that Asian Americans were the "New Jews," a comparison that drives me crazy given that the holistic admissions process of today is a wholly different ballgame than it was during the time of anti-Jewish quotas. But yes, the idea of Asian Americans as the New Jews has caught on because, you know, if it rhymes, it must be true! A quick Google search for "Ron Unz Asian Americans" shows articles in the *New York Times*, *Chicago Tribune*, *Cornell Sun*, *Boston Globe*, *Chronicle of Higher Education*, *Forbes.com*, *Atlantic*, and a slew of other publications. While not all of these pieces espouse agreement with Unz, I list them to show how the article—which is full of painfully faulty logic—played a role in seeding the ground for an anti–affirmative action campaign spearheaded by a portion of the Asian American community. The availability cascade was at work as more and more voices chimed in. (And if more people are saying something, it must be true, right? C'mon, you know better than that.)

The anti-SCA-5 movement launched in 2014 and played a significant role in making Espenshade and Radford's work, as well as Ron Unz's spurious claims, go viral. In November of that same year, Students for Fair Admissions (SFFA) filed their lawsuit against Harvard University. The cascade was in full swing. Since then there has been a back-and-forth between the anti– and pro–affirmative action camps of the Asian American community. When the anti camp presented a statement with sixty signatories, the pro camp came back with 135 organizations signing on supporting affirmative action.[36] Despite the seeming groundswell of Asian American opposition to affirmative action, national polling data continue to indicate that the majority of Asian Americans support affirmative action.[37]

MORE THAN TEST SCORES AND CLASS RANK: THE IMPORTANCE OF HOLISTIC ADMISSIONS FOR ASIAN AMERICANS (AND EVERYONE ELSE)

The dominant narrative is that affirmative action and holistic admissions hurt Asian Americans. But can they help them? More specifically, can affirmative action and holistic admissions practices help Asian Americans who have special traits and talents gain acceptance? The beauty of a system where there are no SAT minimum scores is that it leaves the door open for Asian American students (or any student) who may not have the 1600 but show potential beyond their ability to ace a standardized test. There are no minimum SAT scores to get into an institution—SAT scores are just one part of a bigger package.

On average, Asian Americans applying to elite institutions have relatively high test scores, but that isn't always the case. Harvard alum Jeff Yang wrote an op-ed for CNN.com about how he and his younger sister were able to sneak a look at their files, thanks to his sister's on-campus job in Harvard's admissions office.[38] Yang's sister was miffed to find that, despite her strong grades and high test scores, she was a "marginal" admit and had been bumped over the line because she had an older brother already enrolled and in good standing. Interestingly, Yang's test scores and grades were lower than his sister's. So what got him into Harvard in the first place?

> What saved my application was the optional interview I'd done on campus, in which I'd ended up talking about everything that wasn't in my application: My aspirations to be a writer. The horror movie that I'd scripted and shot in secret at our high school. The subtle

> differences between anxiety, suspense and fear. The fact that I actually really, really suck at piano. The interviewer made the case that I had intangibles that made me a potential asset to the student body, and pressed for me to be considered seriously, despite my middling distinction. Someone decided to take his advice. I hope they didn't end up regretting it.

Yang went on to start *A Magazine*, the first magazine covering Asian Americans with national distribution in major retailers, and he now writes a column for the *Wall Street Journal*. I'd say that Harvard made a good call.

Likewise, I remember the surprise at my own suburban high school every year when we found out if anyone made it into the "big-H." Rarely was the honoree someone who fit the "perfect test score, valedictorian" profile of the students highlighted in the *SFFA v. Harvard* lawsuit, although Asian Americans were definitely among the admitted. My sister's close friend Eddie, multiracial Vietnamese in heritage, was one of them. When talking about the most studious kids in the class, my sister never mentioned Eddie. But when it came to who was the most creative and unconventional, he was definitely mentioned. He wasn't without conventional accomplishments, but he was about as far away from the valedictorian/community service machine/piano excelling profile as you could imagine.[39] Today he's an actor and producer in LA. In my brother's senior year, it was a South Asian guy named Praveen. Not the valedictorian, but a genuinely curious guy. Google tells me that he's a professor at a medical school now. And in my senior year, a lovely White woman named Michelle Knapp was admitted. Michelle was quiet, quirky, and on the down low—brilliant. She never trumpeted her accomplishments and wasn't in the very top cluster of students when it came to class rank, so we were all a little surprised when she got in. Later, as I heard updates about her life, I realized how unique she was: after Harvard, she began a PhD program where her primary research interest was small mammals, in particular bats. Sadly, she passed away in 2006.

And let's not forget many folks' favorite Harvard alum, Jeremy Lin, who ended up with a 4.2 GPA in high school and according to Google anywhere from a 1430 (not counting the writing section) to a 2140 on the SAT.[40] Either way, it adds up to about 710–720 per section. Nice marks, sure, but probably middle of the pack for Harvard admits and below the average of about 2300 for Asian Americans.[41] But honestly, who cares? He's Jeremy Lin! I give these examples to show that, contrary to popular belief, the valedictorian or perfect test taker isn't always who elite institutions like Harvard are looking for. But if you read the complaint filed by SFFA, the message sent is: How could Harvard even think to turn down students who have such perfect credentials?

"Applicant" is the representative put forth by SFFA in their complaint against Harvard for being denied admission to the 2014 entering class. "Applicant" was the valedictorian of their graduating class and had a perfect score (36) on the ACT. "Applicant" was also a National Merit Semi-Finalist, scored perfect 800s on two SAT IIs (Math and History), fundraised for NPR, tutored fellow high schoolers, and volunteered at a tennis camp. An impressive resume, no question. But does it guarantee admission to Harvard?

Here's some context to lend some perspective. A perfect 800 on a SAT II is impressive, but 19 percent of all test takers got a perfect 800 on the Math II SAT in 2015.[42] National Merit Semi-Finalists are great, but there were 16,227 of them in 2015. In case you were wondering, the first-years in Harvard's Class of 2021 numbered 1,694, meaning that the university could, in theory, fill its first-year class almost ten times over with just National Merit Semi-Finalists.[43] While fund-raising, tutoring, and volunteering are all great activities, there's no way to understand the depth or uniqueness of what "Applicant" accomplished. I don't doubt that "Applicant" is an amazing kid. But in this age, when elite college admissions has become an arms race, this type of resume doesn't make them a shoo-in for anything but the honors program at the local state institution (where they could no doubt get an excellent education). Although it's a reality, this is hard news to swallow.

The truth is, in 2017, for the Class of 2021, Harvard admitted only 5.2 percent of applicants.[44] Yes, let's read that again. 5.2 percent. Stanford admitted just 4.8 percent in 2016.[45] Princeton only 6.5 percent.[46] Flagship state institutions have also become much more competitive. Growing up, it was a joke that you could get into our largest state institution if you had a pulse. No one even called it a flagship back then—it was just big. Now it's much more competitive; in pursuit of prestige and an aura of selectivity, many flagship state schools have increased their out-of-state and international student enrollments, which has resulted in more people paying out-of-state tuition and, therefore, tougher standards for the overall applicant pool. So yes, it's a different world today when it comes to admissions, and the downside is that there are going to be a lot of disappointed students out there. But at the same time, we know that talent comes in all sorts of shapes and sizes, including but not limited to test scores—and holistic admissions allows universities to look at the full picture of a student.

THE WHITE QUESTION: OR, IS WHITE RIGHT?

As I see it, many Asian Americans are less upset at the idea that the average SAT scores of African Americans, Latinx, Native Americans, and Asian Americans differ at elite institutions and more miffed at the idea that Whites may receive some advantage over them. This may be because the differences between Asian Americans and URM students are relatively slight. At Harvard, the point differential per section (i.e., Verbal or Math) between Asian Americans and the following groups was 44 points out of 800 for Latinx students, 64 points out of 800 for African American students, and 52 points out of 800 for Native American students.[47] Pretty similar to the point differential if you compared Jeremy Lin's SAT scores to that of the average Asian American at Harvard—not bad at all. It also doesn't take a rocket scientist to see that educational opportunity for these groups, on average, differs so widely.

What probably bothers some Asian Americans more is the allegation that Asian Americans are being disadvantaged or discriminated against as compared to Whites. This is a very delicate matter and one that I don't take lightly as someone who is Asian American and deeply committed to the community. I want my Chinese Korean American child to have the best shot possible to attend the college of his choice.[48] However, after careful review and re-review, I am confident that the data often referenced to prove evidence of discrimination against Asian Americans are inadequate to support such claims.[49] In other words, be cautious when reading the writing of people who claim otherwise, like Ron Unz, 80-20, and Students for Fair Admissions.

The big question remains: Is there negative action against Asian Americans in the college admissions process? *Negative action*, coined by UCLA School of Law professor Jerry Kang, describes the phenomenon of Asian Americans being denied admission from an institution when Whites with equal credentials and qualifications are admitted—basically, the idea that Asian Americans are being discriminated against in favor of Whites.[50] It isn't the same as *affirmative action*, which refers to efforts to broaden opportunity for highly qualified URM applicants. When it comes to affirmative action, Asian Americans aren't being displaced en masse by any of these groups because, let's be real, there aren't enough URM students to begin with. The anti–affirmative action folks would like you to believe that "Asians aren't getting in" because masses of African American, Latinx, and Native American students are; but, sad to say, the combined percentage of these groups is somewhere in the range of 12–18 percent of a student body at most selective institutions—and that's in a good scenario. (Remember that there are places like UC San Diego or UC Irvine where the Black student population is in the range of 1–3 percent. Yes, 1 to 3 percent.) In contrast, White student enrollment tends to be upward of 40–70 percent of a student body; this majority presence means there are many more opportunities to bump Asian Americans out of contention. What we're really talking about here is the potential effects of negative action, not affirmative action.

When Professor Kang wrote his seminal article in 1996, it was a lot easier to prove and document negative action. The selective public system with the highest number of Asian Americans was the University of California system, which used a point-based system to admit applicants. Students received points for having certain SAT scores, GPAs, special traits, and the like. You added up the points and had a pretty good sense of whether you could get in. The formula model efficiently managed the needs of the gigantic UC system. Under this approach to admissions, it would be especially easy to spot if Asian Americans were getting in at significantly lower rates than Whites, because the criteria included in any comparison were the only criteria under consideration. Today, however, the UC system uses a comprehensive holistic review for its admissions, one similar to the process used at selective, elite private institutions. There is no longer a point-based formula (those went out with the *Gratz* ruling), and there are many more criteria being considered: essays and teacher recommendations are scrutinized much more carefully, the quality of extracurricular accomplishments is evaluated and not just tallied, etc. Because of this nuanced process, negative action is much more difficult to diagnose in a system that uses a holistic review of students. This is why Espenshade said that his finding that Asian Americans had, on average, SAT scores that were 140 points lower than White admittees does not conclusively prove discrimination against Asian Americans. There are too many other factors that could contribute to why Asian Americans who hit a certain test score threshold may not be getting in at the same exact rate as their White peers.[51] Remember, there is no magic test score that guarantees admissions for anyone.

Other claims that Asian Americans are being rampantly discriminated against in college admissions fall short. Simply put, the evidence isn't there, and the data that folks are using to make these claims are insufficient. For instance, in the complaint filed by SFFA against Harvard, proposed evidence compares the percentage of Asian Americans at a place like California Institute of Technology (Caltech) versus Harvard. Caltech does have a higher percentage of Asian Americans, but we aren't comparing apples to apples here.[52] If you couldn't tell from the name—Caltech is a science- and technology-oriented institution, while Harvard has a whole array of majors (or "concentrations," as they like to call them). While not all Asian Americans do well at science and math, enough of them excel to make up a sizeable proportion of an elite math and science university, surprise surprise. In its complaint, SFFA also noted how the Asian American percentages at the elite public high schools in New York City—Stuyvesant, Hunter College High School, and the like—are higher than the equivalent percentages at Harvard.[53] But, once again, there's a different metric at play. The NYC system admits are solely based on performance on the Specialized High School Admissions Test, while elite colleges use a holistic review system that considers not only test scores but a myriad of other traits. In fact, the NYC public high school admissions process is often criticized for being too rigid for only taking test scores into account, although this may change.[54]

Another example of SFFA's flawed logic comes in a series of examples that note how Asian Americans make up a larger percentage of the applicant pool than present in the student body. For instance, they cite an article written by Richard Sander, a professor at UCLA School of Law, who has spent recent years claiming that underrepresented minority groups are mismatched to elite institutions.[55] We'll hear more about his work later. Sander looked at who students were sending their SAT score reports to. The study found that for three of the most selective Ivy League institutions, 27 percent of score senders were Asian Americans. SFFA pounced, citing in their complaint Sander's claim that "over this same time period, however, Asian Americans represented only 17–20% of the admitted students. No other racial or ethnic group at these schools is as underrepresented relative to its application numbers as are Asian Americans."[56]

My response is, And . . . so? Just because a group sends its score reports at a higher rate than other groups doesn't guarantee that it would be represented at the same rate in the final group of admittees. Last time I checked, all it took to send score reports was checking a box. (This generation of kids probably clicks a drop-down menu or something.) While many, many Asian Americans aren't even thinking about Harvard (remember, 40 percent attend community colleges), many are. It's just in the Kool-Aid for a sizable subset of Asian Americans. These are brand-name universities that are the stuff of legends—if not to the kids, to their dreaming parents—and a lot of high schoolers, ranging from highly qualified to laughably unqualified, are going to send their scores or submit an application.[57] These days with the Common App, all it takes is just writing another check for the application fee.

But the folks suing Harvard aren't convinced. In case you didn't get where they were going with all of this, the SFFA complaint reads: "Thus, if Harvard admitted randomly from its applicant pool, the number of Asian Americans . . . would be higher than it actually is."[58] But why would Harvard admit randomly from its applicant pool? Selective college admissions isn't a raffle where the more tickets you buy is congruent with the chance of success.

To draw a parallel, I chaired admissions for my graduate program for a number of years. We're a pretty competitive program, admitting about 10 to 20 percent of master's applicants, which means that we turn away a lot of amazing folks—we have to. Because these graduate school applicants want to work in a university setting, a lot of them have the similar profile. To estimate, probably about one-third every year were leaders in their Greek-life group during college, and this is fairly consistent year to year. So does that mean that in our final group of admittees, 30 percent of them will be former fraternity or sorority officers? Absolutely not. We look for the strongest applicants who we think have the most potential to come together and create a vibrant learning community. Some years there are a number of Greeks, yes, but other years there are none. There is no commitment to any group at a certain rate based on their representation in the applicant pool.

Going back to the lawsuit, so of course Espenshade, Espenshade, Espenshade comes up in the SFFA complaint—the supposed 140 points that Asian Americans "need" to get in anywhere. Well let's play their game and look at the fuller picture painted by Espenshade and friends. Oddly, something that people never mention when they talk about this study is the finding that low-income and working-class Asian Americans are *significantly more likely to be admitted*, as are other low-income students of color. Instead, the story that people have taken from the study is that, with the exception of Asian Americans, racial minorities are getting a bump in admissions and low-income students are not. This interpretation has led to many decisive claims that race-conscious admissions hurts low-income students writ large.

However, if people actually looked at the study's data (pages 85–86 for anyone toting their own personal copy of Espenshade and Radford's *No Longer Separate, Not Yet Equal*), they would see that there's a more complex story being told.[59] Espenshade and Radford's analysis uses interaction effects to see if any sort of significant effect was associated with the combinations (or intersections between) of being Black and low income, Black and working class, Latinx and low income, Asian American and low income, and the like. In recent years, *intersectionality* has entered the popular vernacular as people are becoming more aware that there's something unique about a woman of color versus just a "woman," for example. Interaction effects are statistics' way of trying to capture these intersections and see if there's any effect associated with being, for instance, Black and low income versus just Black or just low income.

And oh there is. There in broad daylight, Espenshade and Radford's findings show that low-income Black, Latinx, and Asian Americans all have a significantly higher chance of admissions at private institutions than do White students writ large when looking just at standardized admissions metrics. Breaking it down, the authors explain:

> The [socioeconomic] gradient for nonwhite students at private schools consistently favors candidates from lower and working class backgrounds over those from more privileged circumstances . . . There is strong support for the view that admission officers are awarding extra weight to nonwhite students from poor and working-class families—especially those who are at closest to the bottom of the income distribution . . . For nonwhite students, on the other hand, there are clear signs of a low [socioeconomic] admissions advantage. Black students who come from lower or working class backgrounds can expect a favorable admissions decision in 87 percent and 53 percent of their cases, respectively. The expected chance of being admitted falls to just 17 percent for upper-class Black students. Strikingly similar patterns characterize chances by social class for Hispanic and Asian applicants to private institutions.[60]

According to the data, the likelihood of admission for the group of Asian Americans from the lowest income bracket at private institutions is 58 percent, 30 percent for working-class Asian Americans, and only 10–17 percent for higher-income Asian Americans.[61]

If you're opposed to any form of race-conscious admissions, you may still be perturbed that the probability of a low-income Black student being admitted is still higher than that for a low-income Asian American. That trend exists in large part because of how very few low-income Black students there are competing at the level of elite college admissions due to rampant educational inequality. They really are unicorns. But if you're concerned that race-conscious admissions hurts Asian Americans in a way that especially penalizes those from low-income and working-class backgrounds, Espenshade and Radford show that these Asian American students are actually receiving a boost; they have a significantly *higher* likelihood of admission than their test scores, GPA, and other standardized metrics would predict. Yes, they are still outnumbered by upper-middle-class Asian Americans in selective institutions overall, but of those who do apply to elite private institutions, it appears that they receive special consideration.

Confession: When I stumbled on these findings, which were there all along in plain view—not buried in some footnote—I was stunned, and a little embarrassed. I had already spent a good amount of time highlighting my copy of Espenshade and critiquing the false assumption that Asian Americans need higher test scores to get in. How did I miss this finding that blows that assumption out of the water? My confession is that I'm subject to the same cognitive biases and stereotypes of my own racial/ethnic groups that others are. I have the dubious honor of falling victim to the *bias blind spot*, a term that captures the cognitive bias of seeing how biases affect others' judgment but failing to recognize that I myself am affected by bias.[62] Basically, we tend to think everyone else is more biased than ourselves and to think that we're the accurate ones. Au contraire! But how does someone who studies this stuff for a living miss the critical finding that low-income Asian Americans receive some benefit at elite private institutions?

With the media—social, print, and otherwise—making a big deal of the "140 points" headline, the fuller story got lost in the frenzy. Perhaps because the finding so powerfully reinforces entrenched stereotypes about Asian Americans that many harbor, that they excel at standardized tests, I (and many others) just stopped looking for another story. It's shocking, sobering, and fascinating all at once. At least I'm in good company. Espenshade and Radford note how other analyses by super smart folks like William Bowen, the former president of Princeton, and others also missed the preferences given to low-income students of color because they neglected to tease out the patterns between public versus private institutions, thus contributing to the false perception that low-income students unequivocally lose out under a race-conscious system.[63] I'm a little embarrassed to miss some important data, but it's a good reminder that we're all subject to blind spots and biases. Hopefully I get some slack for owning up to it.[64]

ATHLETES AND LEGACIES: A WHITE ADMISSIONS ADVANTAGE, BUT DIFFERENT FROM AFFIRMATIVE ACTION

Obviously, there is a lot more than the SAT that matters in admissions. But because the "Asians are discriminated against" camp makes so much of the supposed SAT disadvantage that Asian Americans receive, let's look more closely at scores. According to the complaint filed against Harvard, the average SAT score (for the version of the test with a maximum score of 2400) for "East Asians and Indians" in the entering class of 2017 was 2299. (Side note: This average specifically leaves out Southeast Asian American students, who often receive special consideration under race-conscious admissions policies, again challenging the claim that Asian Americans are hurt under affirmative action.) The average listed for African Americans was 2107 and for Native Americans 2142.[65] I disagree with SFFA's claim that these scores vary "widely"; the "great variation" ends up being just 44 points per section for Latinx, 52 points for Native Americans, and 64 points for African Americans. Sure, it's the difference between a 730 and a 780 on a section, but I wouldn't say that anyone is rampantly unqualified.

If we really want to see if there's systemic discrimination based on SAT scores, our real target of scrutiny is the White–Asian American comparison. For Whites (conveniently not listed in the complaint, for some reason), the score gap ends up being 22 points per section on average for the Class of 2017. However, consider that potentially an estimated 33–40 percent of the White student population at Harvard are legacies or recruited athletes, both groups that can receive special consideration in the admissions system.[66] That is a lot of students who may be evaluated through a special lens. I'm not saying these students are slackers—to only have a 22-points-per-section gap with Asian Americans, who surely have a much smaller representation of legacies and recruited athletes in their midst, is pretty impressive. There are some smart lacrosse or whatever-they-play players walking around Cambridge. Another caveat is that likely many (hopefully) of these students are outstanding regardless of their status as legacies or athletes, so they aren't necessarily only being admitted because of this factor. Nevertheless, legacy or athletic consideration can shape admissions.

The special consideration context that some White students receive likely explains any point gap between Asian Americans and Whites. In fact, if you had only non-legacies and nonathletes, I wouldn't be surprised if Whites outscored the aggregate Asian American group. Sorry aunties who send your kids to cram school; but hey, the silver lining is that the SAT is just a number! So yes, I am glad that elite institutions look at more than numbers. The high SAT scores are a semi-necessary but totally insufficient condition. I mean, you are competing with some of the smartest lacrosse players in the world (hopefully). But the point is, almost everyone who ends up at Harvard is pretty smart. Yes, there are duds who shall remain nameless, but for the most part it's a bright bunch.

BREATHE. YOUR LIFE WILL BE FINE WITHOUT HARVARD

Many kids, especially a sizeable number of Asian Americans, grow up hearing, "Study hard and you'll get into Harvard." But being pretty awesome and good at taking tests doesn't really make you stand out in the Harvard applicant pool. When admit rates are as low as 5 percent and dropping, it's not even a question of "the best and brightest" anymore; it is more like "a certain number of exceptionally great students." Yet every subsequent generation seems to receive more socialization into the idea that they are a special snowflake; and yes, the stories of the Asian American kids who had good test scores and were valedictorian who didn't get into Harvard are a little sad.

But remember, number 1, there may be some other Asian kid who got in who wasn't valedictorian but did some really crazy, unique things and is now on the path to doing even greater things. And number 2, if you're already a good student, you are going to end up just fine. I know because I was one of those kids.

My husband teases me for deciding to broadcast the fact that I didn't get into Harvard in the *Washington Post* (go big or go home), but it's true.[67] But after years of pretending that I never wanted to go to Harvard and dismissively saying that I wasn't even going to apply, I, uh, secretly sent in an application. I wasn't valedictorian, but I had a decent SAT score, and my high school had a track record of quirky nonvaledictorians being admitted. Maybe I was next! Well, spoiler alert, I didn't get in. But I sent in a last-minute application to Vanderbilt and one day received a surprise phone call telling me that not only did I get in but I'd landed the Chancellor's Scholarship, which was back then a scholarship for racial minorities.[68] Never mind that I had never stepped foot into the state of Tennessee; they had me at "free tuition." Vanderbilt was one of the few top-ranked schools that still aggressively recruited Asian Americans (I found that many of my friends had been wooed with similarly generous financial aid packages) and there was a reason for this: Vanderbilt needed all the diversity it could get. Vanderbilt also was the first campus to sponsor the renowned Posse program, which brings urban youth to college campuses that they otherwise would not have ended up at. We used to joke that our campus didn't know how to handle diversity, but it did know how to spend money to get students of color.

Although I received an excellent education, the campus climate was challenging. We're talking about a place that didn't rename Confederate Memorial Hall until well into the twenty-first century. I did, however, have an amazing time working with the Asian American Student Association in collaboration with the other student groups supporting diversity. Vanderbilt reminds me that race-conscious admissions can look very different from campus to campus. It allowed one campus that desperately needed racial minority students, including Asian Americans, to actively recruit them. Harvard didn't need me, but Vanderbilt did. In the fall of 2016, the Asian American population at Vanderbilt was 12.6 percent, which might sound low if you're from California but is absolutely mind-blowingly high to me—it's basically double the percent of when I was there. And those of us who stuck it out during those hard times are part of why it has more diversity today.[69] Like other elite privates, race-conscious admissions is essential not just for encouraging places like Vanderbilt to recruit diversity but for actively countering the historical legacy of exclusion and inequality that permeates its past and present.

So yes, Asian American kids who didn't go to Harvard: If you are as accomplished and interesting as your college applications say, you are going to be just fine. Something noteworthy is that due to anonymity, we have no remaining information on where "Applicant" eventually enrolled or was admitted. It's possible that they're happily walking the gorges of Ithaca at Cornell or partying at a Dartmouth frat house or singing in an acapella group at Amherst. Or maybe they're in the honors program at a state university. All we know from the SFFA lawsuit is that they didn't get into Harvard.[70] But I'm pretty sure they're doing just fine.

CHAPTER FIVE

Why the SAT and SAT Prep Fall Short

IN MY LITTLE BUBBLE of upper-middle-class kids who took AP classes, a lot of hype existed around the importance of a good SAT score. There was early signaling galore. I have a distant memory of being no older than seven or eight and seeing my sister's friend, who was maybe twelve, receive a SAT study book from her mother, along with a stern minilecture on how she had better make good use of the book. Our high school archived photos of the year's National Merit Semifinalists in an award showcase near the front of the school. Bored and waiting for my mom to pick me up, I would flip through the large photo sheets and recognize the usual suspects of my older brother's and sister's friends who excelled academically. I remember my brother's middle-of-the-day phone call his junior year. Nearly out of breath, he asked me to open his mail and read aloud the scores next to the Math and Verbal sections. I had no idea what the numbers meant at the time, but when he sounded happy, I knew they were good.

These messages are sent early and often: this test matters. Over time, I came to know both what a good score was and what a less desirable score was. When my time came to take the PSAT, I picked up a few books and started doing the repetitive exercises. I (almost) made it through a few practice tests, half-heartedly made flashcards, and wondered why I needed to worry so much about this dumb test. At some extremely nerdy and competitive subconscious level, I wanted to be in that photo showcase like my siblings before me. Well, that dream sure tanked; my score was okay but unexceptional.

I puttered on to prepare for the SAT. My practice test scores, when I could muster up the motivation to actually calculate them, were in an okay-not-exceptional range. When the big day finally came during the spring of my junior year (a beautiful day spent inside with a No. 2 pencil), I went in less stressed than I'd been for the PSAT—there was no photo showcase for the actual SAT, and I knew I could retake the test in the fall. Using my tried and true standardized test trick (if you don't know it quickly, skip it and come back to it) and a few other strategies, I gamely powered through. By some truly divine miracle, my actual score ended up being about two hundred points higher than what I'd scored on practice tests. It made me more competitive for the scholarship that eventually sent me to college, and it definitely influenced my sense of what was possible when I applied to schools.

Contrast my experience with the students at low-income high schools in the Chicago Public Schools system described in Regina Deil-Amen and Tenisha Tevis's excellent article "Circumscribed Agency: The Relevance of Standardized College Entrance Exams for Low SES High School Students."[1] Many of these students had little idea of how to interpret test scores. They also didn't know that they could retake the test to try to get a better score and had little sense that this was a test that people extensively prepared for. Although these students were bright and talented, Kumon and Princeton Review were not part of their vernacular.

Valuing education is not exclusive to any one racial/ethnic group. This is evidenced in research which shows that African American students have higher educational expectations than White students.[2] Refuting stereotypes that they dismiss education due to associations with Whiteness ("acting White"), students of color generally understand that education is critical.[3] Very few people grow up thinking that they really don't want to make anything of themselves. But communities have dramatically different options when it comes to being able to turn those hopes into a concrete reality. If you thought the discrepancy between my experience and the experience of low-income high schoolers in Chicago is disturbing, consider that I didn't even engage in a formal test prep course for which people pony up anywhere from a few hundred to a few thousand dollars.

The test prep industry is an entrenched and pervasive presence in the lives of the upper middle class, as well as within some East Asian American subgroups. Usually discussions around inequality and test prep focus on the discrepancies in access, which is a natural place to start given the gap between the haves and the have-nots. But the conversation needs to push further. In this chapter, in addition to covering unequal test prep access, we are going to discuss a lesser-known driver of inequality in standardized testing—the issue of *who* benefits from test prep. Understanding the underlying conditions for why there are inequitable benefits derived from test prep helps us question the utility of the big test itself as an effective "sorting hat" (to borrow from *Harry Potter*) for the postsecondary pathways of college students. To drive all that home, we'll look at some of the outcomes of institutions that have gone SAT optional and consider what the research on SAT prep (and who benefits) says about how standardized test scores are viewed and used both in college admissions and by individuals trying to understand who "deserves" to attend a certain college.

WHO TAKES TEST PREP?

We begin our depressing journey toward understanding how inequality around the SAT is even worse than what you thought it was in a very pleasant place: the San Gabriel Valley of greater Los Angeles, a place filled with sunshine and great food. As you drive around the LA 'burbs of Monterey Park, Alhambra, and Rowland Heights, you can't miss the signs on local businesses that showcase side-by-side Chinese-English translations. While there's a class divide between places like wealthy San Marino (which my old roommate called "Chan Marino") and the more economically diverse areas of the San Gabriel Valley, there is a common experience that unites many local youth: test prep. Whether it's Kaplan, Princeton Review, or one of the cram schools with a storefront sign that shouts its services in multiple languages, an estimated 42 percent of all Chinese American students nationwide will take a SAT prep course prior to college. In the Korean American community, it's even higher at 50.7 percent.[4]

While higher-income Chinese Americans are notably more likely to take SAT prep than their low-income peers (a 19.4 percentage point gap), the class divide in the Korean American community is less apparent: 55.4 percent of wealthier Korean Americans and 46.7 percent of low-income Korean Americans still take it. In starker terms, low-income Korean Americans are more likely than rich White kids (42.0 percent) to take SAT prep.[5] And these stats are twenty years old, from a time when SAT prep was becoming more common and when selective and elite college admissions was less of an arms race. Today, even more kids nationwide are spending their summers hammering away at Kumon.

In New York City, the frenzy starts even earlier. Test prep businesses for the Specialized High School Admissions Test, which determines who gets into the city's selective public high schools, are plentiful in ethnic communities, with some businesses boasting their talents in Korean, Chinese, and Russian—all on one sign at street level. (You have to wonder if the translations are more for the parents than the kids.) The composition of the selective high schools reflects the makeup of the test prep market: in 2011, while 17 percent of eighth graders in the NYC Public Schools were Asian American, at the high schools where admittance is contingent on an exam score Asian Americans made up 57 percent of the student body.[6]

Test prep in the East Asian American community exists in a unique ecosystem. Immigrant parents come from countries where college admissions is based on a single test score, so afterschool test prep is all but standard for anyone hoping to go to college. (I recommend the Korean drama *Answer Me 1988* for an apt depiction, great show.) The ethnic economy supports these expectations through the existence of a test prep industry specifically advertised to ethnic youth. With a range of options that cater to varying levels of affordability, from being crammed in a classroom with fifty-plus students to one-on-one tutoring, test prep can be more accessible than it is in other communities. Economies of scale and basic competition drive prices down as well. And the ethnic community also provides venues where low-, middle-, and upper-income immigrants and their children mix, like churches, temples, ethnic grocery stores, and so on. So while everyone in the community may not be best friends, the phenomenon of everyone being more or less stuck together helps reduce the information isolation that low-income families are highly susceptible to. So a low-income mom working in a Chinese beauty salon may observe that everyone is sending their kid to afterschool SAT classes. She sees advertisements in the ethnic newspaper that brag about the colleges that local kids are getting into and becomes determined to find some way to send Junior off to a class or a summer program. It doesn't always happen that way, but it happens enough that 31.8 percent of low-income Chinese Americans take SAT prep.[7]

While social class still certainly divides opportunity for East Asian Americans, there are some unique forces that help buffer the effect of class.[8] When it comes to the rest of the United States, however, social class matters in even starker ways. Without a strong, race/ethnicity-targeted lifelong messaging campaign that S-A-T are the three most important letters in the alphabet (socialization into a set of cognitive schemas affecting East Asian Americans that sociologists Jennifer Lee and Min Zhou call "the success frame"), these messages more naturally drift up to the folks for whom plunking down a few thousand dollars for a test prep class and a private college counselor sounds logical, versus a completely insane idea.[9] When you have families who expect to pay full price for tuition, room, and board, what's another few extra thousand to make sure that Junior can get into the best school possible?

It all boils down to the basic idea that the actions people take make sense in their own heads, and that sense of what is normal, rational, and possible is shaped by the forces of social class—what pioneering theorist Pierre Bourdieu calls one's "habitus," one's own little bubble, or force field—which explains why certain thoughts that make perfect sense to one person or group make absolutely no sense to another.[10] Private summer camps, private college counselors, expensive SAT prep courses, and, in a good number of cases, private school (especially for people who already live in good school districts—I really don't get that one) are part of the habitus of the wealthy and a good portion of the upper middle class.

"JUST EXPAND ACCESS": A CASE OF BIKESHEDDING

Inequality in test prep access is often presented as a simple story: rich kids and certain racial/ethnic groups have access to test prep, but other groups do not. The proposed solution is that if other groups had access, educational inequality would be solved, or at least be greatly reduced. This approach reflects an interesting cognitive bias when it comes to people's thinking on how to solve the SAT equity issue. The policy solution of "just expand access" is an example of Parkinson's law of triviality, also known as *bikeshedding*, which proposes that organizations tend to dedicate more time and favor toward simple solutions that are easy to grasp and that resonate with a broad audience of people, instead of more complex approaches. Parkinson's 1957 example of the law at work has a fictional committee deciding among three funding proposals: a £10 million contract to build a nuclear reactor, a £350 contract to build a bike shed for the staff, and a £21 budget to buy snacks for the committee (mmm, snacks).[11] In the end, the bike shed wins—it's tangible, doable, and easy to understand. Hence the term *bikeshedding*. Likewise, expanding SAT prep is easy to understand and get on board with. The obvious problem is that rich kids have access to SAT prep and poor kids don't. So let's give low-income kids access and then everything will be solved! Donor checks written, summer programs set up, and voila; we have a solution. We get the educational equivalent of a shiny new bike shed but are still limited in addressing systemic inequality.

Expanding prep will help some students; but in terms of making a big difference writ large, the type that shows up as a statistically significant effect, well, it doesn't appear to be working in the ways that one would predict.[12] Inequality in test prep access affects different sets of students in different ways, and "test prep for all" is an overly simplistic and incomplete answer to a very complex problem. First, there's inequality in both affordability and availability to consider, which could be assisted by broadening access to test prep. But there's also inequality in effectiveness, which means that "test prep for all" is too little too late. Let's take a closer look at both.

INEQUALITY IN ACCESS

Test prep stratifies inequality first by bolstering the test scores of academically talented students who have access to its services—and this group tends to be disproportionately upper income and/or East Asian American. This phenomenon has resulted in an admissions "arms race," where a 1200 or a 1300 isn't considered competitive at a top-tier institution and so students feel the pressure to get their score up to the 1400–1500 range. It's not that the students become magically smarter in six months; but with enough discipline and familiarity with test-taking techniques, scores for (some) people can go up.

My (Taiwanese American) husband is a good example. Growing up in the competitive suburbs of Potomac, Maryland, he signed up for SAT prep before his senior year, even though his previous scores were strong. The Princeton Review class he attended separated students out by prior achievement level, so there was a whole class of those who initially scored in the 1400s or so who aspired to cut into the 1500s by mastering test prep strategies. Reflecting on his experience, he observed that there was a huge difference between students who took test prep to acquire fundamental knowledge (less effective) and those who were mainly learning strategies to get their scores to the next level (more effective).

So there's a traffic jam toward the upper end of the achievement bell curve, resulting in students enduring the anxiety and stress of tight competition and everyone feeling a bit more miserable, because who wants to spend the last summer of high school studying for a test? Additionally, the test score arms race negatively impacts opportunity for low-income students. While low-income students of color receive special consideration in the admissions process, at private institutions at least, there's no telling who's counting themselves out of the competition because of the perception that lower test scores won't cut it, on top of the other forces already discouraging low-income students from applying to more selective (and pricey) institutions.[13]

The test score arms race also means that we aren't necessarily comparing apples to apples when we look at SAT scores. The entire point of the test is to be a standardized measure that compares and ranks scores. Instead, you get clusters of scores at the high range, but it's impossible to know who gained that score with or without extensive test prep. As the continued controversy over affirmative action shows, admissions counselors have some knowledge that low-income and underrepresented minority students are more likely to fall into the "no or little" test prep category, but the public also makes tremendous judgments about who deserves to attend a certain college based on test scores.

The other key way that test prep access stratifies opportunity for students is that it serves as a means for the average/above average but not spectacular higher-income student to get ahead. What happens to the middle 40 percent of the population is a huge part of inequality. You figure that the top echelon—the top 10–20 percent of academically bright youth—are going to be mostly okay, whatever happens. Yes, it's unfair that smart low-income students often don't get the extra support that they could benefit from. There's no question that being wealthy and in the top 10 percent gets you a lot more opportunities than being low-income and in the top academic stratum.[14] But across the socioeconomic spectrum, these kids are bright, conscientious, and self-motivated enough to do their homework and do it well, which is a huge part of making it to the top 20 percent of anything. After all, half of the game is just showing up day after day. I'm painting with very broad brushstrokes, I know; certainly there's a lot of underdeveloped and underutilized talent in that top 20 percent, and many bright kids still fall through the cracks. But on the whole there are probably more opportunities for the top 20 percent of lower-income academic achievers than there are for their peers who are more in the middle-achiever category.

Highly worrisome is what happens to that second, and to some extent the third, quartile, where we see the even more pernicious and cumulative consequences of inequality. Well-off but academically average-ish students have far more safety nets and opportunities than a student who is academically average and low-income. An academically average or even below-average kid with financial means can get sent to test prep or tutoring, hire a private college counselor to all but write their essay, and end up at a four-year university. And they'll have their parents to lean on as they make their way into the world and find a decent enough job that provides financial security.

An academically average or below-average student from a low-income background has very few of these potential opportunities and is at risk of getting swept up in postsecondary plans with few safety nets or second chances when accidents or mistakes happen—the kind that eighteen- and nineteen-year-olds commonly make. If these students are able to attend college, they may struggle to balance classes and work or don't have enough money for books, so they fall behind in studying for a class. They don't know that going to office hours is something that can help you *and* bolster your participation grade, not a sign of weakness.[15] They might get recruited by a predatory for-profit institution that doesn't have their best interests at mind. There's a reason why transfer rates to community college and graduation rates at many four-year institutions are dismally low: all of these "little things" add up.

Extending test prep to low-income students won't radically change this situation. The rich will always have more to fall back on, materially at least, and will have the networks and resources that can help provide a Plan B when Plan A gets messed up. But it's important to recognize how test prep is part of the package of assets and resources that more affluent students—even those who are academically lackluster—leverage to get ahead. The actual impact on a test score for the less academically stellar may be minimal. But in many ways the ability to go to test prep is a proxy for a broader set of advantages that higher-income students are able to utilize. Test prep represents money and the idea that someone is standing behind you, willing to fork over the money to pay for it. It also represents socialization into a world where there's a sequence of events—taking test prep, selecting a list of colleges, making college visits, hiring a college consultant, paying application fees, and the like—that propel one set of students toward four-year institutions. And this is a sequence that not all students experience, or even know about.

So yes, there are tremendous inequities in test prep participation for the especially bright as well as for those who are in the realm of slightly above or below average. Plain and simple: it's not fair that a certain swath of the population can more easily access a valued service that is out of reach for the rest of the population. However, is the solution as simple as just expanding access? The research on who actually benefits from test prep shows how this approach, while well meaning, may fall short in its effectiveness It's a bit of an awkward conversation, but let's go there.

THE LIMITED EFFECTIVENESS OF TEST PREP FOR MOST STUDENTS

Many of us are familiar with the advertising advanced by test prep companies—"Boost your score by 150 to 400 points, guaranteed!" Smiling students clutch their acceptance letters (or email printouts) to their dream schools and offer up testimonials that [insert your favorite company] made all the difference. It's so appealing and seems so convincing. It makes for great advertising; the only issue is that when subjected to more advanced statistical methods, the actual "difference" associated with test prep is much lower: about 10 to 30 points, if any at all.[16] Why the large discrepancy?

Well, a commonsensical but not particularly statistically robust way for people to assess "change" in test scores is to simply compare a pre-test score to a post-test score. So a test prep company will record a student's baseline score with their score after taking the course and will note that—voila!—the second score is higher! But in the world of educational evaluation, this approach doesn't cut it when it comes to making broad claims about whether a program works or not. In a nutshell, the best way to assess whether something is working in this type of context is to have two randomly assigned groups, with only one receiving the intervention. A randomized controlled trial (RCT) is often called the "gold standard" level of evidence in this type of assessment.[17] You know how people like to say things like "correlation is not causality" or, if you're actually a social scientist, "the methods used are unable to indicate causation"? Well, the RCT is the one where traditionally the most social scientists are comfortable saying that it indicates causation, or it's as close as we can get to establishing it.

Be wary when you see claims that something is "working," especially when you see claims of miracles. For instance, the College Board rolled out free tutoring via Khan Academy, a very nice thing. Among students who studied for twenty hours using the tools, there was a reported average "115-point increase between their earlier and preliminary PSAT/NMSQT exam and the actual SAT."[18] Also, the "improvement was reportedly double the average increase of students who did not use the Khan tutorials." Sounds great, right? But beyond the fact that students studied for twenty hours, what sort of factors might have driven those who took advantage of the Khan program versus those who did not? Even if their GPAs and demographic factors were roughly similar, there were likely self-selection factors that motivated some students and not others to take the initiative and sign up for the Khan Academy tutoring. And that means that you're in danger of comparing two very different groups. I'm not saying that the Khan tutoring program is a bad thing (can't argue with free), but instead of claims that it is magically leveling the playing field, a more appropriate claim might be that it's "making the playing field a bit less terrible," which is still no small feat!

So, how do you really know that test prep is working? Is it more a function of self-selection, where certain students are already more academically prepared or motivated? How do you isolate the effect of the treatment? RCTs are not always feasible or realistic to set up, which is why there aren't any solely addressing SAT prep at the time of writing. However, there are better ways to evaluate effectiveness than the pre-/post-test comparison, which doesn't account for the other dynamics that could explain why you see a difference in test scores.

One approach is to get everyone's test scores and other background traits, primarily demographic traits (e.g., race, class, gender, etc.) and academic background (e.g., high school GPA, prior academic achievement). Better yet is to also get measures related to motivation and other constructs that might be linked to self-selection. Throw the data into a computer program and use techniques like regression (the Swiss Army knife of social science statistical research) to hold certain terms constant. Conceptually, you're trying to predict the effect associated with a SAT prep class if everyone in the sample had the same GPA, social class, etc. Using these approaches, Derek Briggs, director of the Center for Assessment Design Research and Evaluation at the University of Colorado Boulder and the father of test prep evaluation research, uncovered that the actual gains associated with test prep for the overall population are much smaller than those espoused by the big companies. Basically, take off a zero and you're closer to the overall bump associated with test prep, ten to thirty points.[19]

Subsequent research on test prep has uncovered similar findings. Not only that, but it's found that Asian American and upper-income students tend to benefit more from test prep.[20] A study by Soo-yong Byun, at Penn State University, Hyunjoon Park, at the University of Pennsylvania, basically found that East Asian Americans were really the only group benefiting from test prep.[21] This study parceled out different racial/ethnic groups for analysis, an approach that can identify inequities between various groups as long as sample size is adequate. Importantly, they separated Chinese, Korean, and Japanese Americans from the overall Asian American population and put them into an "East Asian American" category. They also compared the effects of different types of test preparation (e.g., private tutoring; attending a private course). Their analysis indicated that East Asian Americans were the only group that had significantly higher SAT scores with any type of test prep and that higher scores were only associated with one type of test preparation, taking a private course. In my own work I have seen similar results: there was some effect linked with taking a SAT prep course for the overall population, but Asian Americans were the only group where a significant effect popped up when the different racial/ethnic groups were analyzed separately.[22]

Designing effective RCTs on SAT prep is tricky. Can you ethically administer an expensive treatment (a prep course)—which may or may not be effective but is perceived as a highly valued resource—to one group while giving the other group nothing (which is seen as highly ineffective) or the academic equivalent of a placebo? It's also an expensive experiment, with SAT prep having a value of at least $500–$1,000 per student. The closest thing to a well-designed RCT on SAT prep is an experiment conducted by Christopher Avery, Roy E. Larson Professor of Public Policy at the Harvard Kennedy School of Government.[23] He designed a RCT to evaluate the effectiveness of College Possible, a program that helps prepare low-income and first-generation youth for the college admissions process. As part of the program, students take a SAT/ACT preparation course. On certain outcomes, College Possible demonstrated effectiveness: participation was linked with higher applications to and enrollment in selective four-year institutions. However, when it came to SAT/ACT scores, there were no significant differences between College Possible participants and those who did not participate. While valuable, the study's broader focus was on program participation, versus being an evaluation of SAT prep alone, so there was not a pure control group for the SAT prep part. As Avery noted, although it is unlikely that the control group students participated much in SAT prep, it is possible that they received some sort of tutoring or preparation on their own.

All of this is to say that the overall body of research on SAT prep does not resoundingly support its effectiveness—with the exception of East Asian Americans. An intriguing finding from Byun and Park's study is that East Asian Americans were also the only group where students with higher prior achievement were more likely to take a SAT prep course.[24] This pattern suggests that test prep is more attractive and effective for a particular group of students: those who are already academically strong and likely using test prep to make their scores even more competitive. Thinking back to my husband's test prep experience, there's a big difference between using test prep to move a 1400 to a 1500 versus getting exposed to some of the fundamentals for the first time in a prep course. The playing field is already unequal, and even a season of intensive cramming is unable to undo the cumulative effects of unequal schooling and resources. As alluring as it is, universal test prep is limited in its effectiveness to level the playing field.

Why do East Asian Americans appear to benefit uniquely from SAT prep? No, they aren't magically smarter than everyone else. Rather, and as I explained in the last chapter, it's a unique combination of heavy socialization into the idea that the SAT matters greatly and the high availability of resources that help translate aspirations into realities: (1) relatively high-quality K–12 schooling (while many students still face barriers to their schooling, as an aggregate group, Asian Americans are the most racially integrated minority population in the public school arena); (2) the ethnic economy, which provides a slew of test prep options as well as venues where Asian Americans mix across social class, leading to the flow of information around education; and (3) the ethnic community, which fosters an atmosphere wherein test prep is seen as a normative and even expected behavior. Combine these with what sociologists Lee and Zhou refer to as the "success frame," and you have a potent force that exerts high societal pressure on Asian American students to gain early familiarity with the test.[25]

Other individual students of all races may have *some* access to *some* of these things, but this combination of resources doesn't exist for any other racial/ethnic group writ large in the way that it does for East Asian Americans. For instance, White students' participation in SAT prep course was 35.6 percent in 1997, but in Byun and Park's study participation in SAT prep was not linked with significantly higher scores for White students, or any other group but East Asian Americans.[26] All of this suggests that the minimal gain of ten to thirty points identified by Briggs are being driven by the subsamples of East Asian American students, as well as by already high-achieving and higher-SES students for whom taking SAT prep is linked with significantly higher scores.[27] Several studies have noted lower effects associated with coaching for Black students, particularly on the verbal section, even though rates of participation are surprisingly high for Black students.[28] One study found that while coaching had some positive benefits for Black students on the math section, "the effect on the verbal section of the SAT for Black students was 18 points lower than the coaching effect for non-Black students."[29] So not only is there vast inequality around who gets to take SAT prep, there's also inequity in who benefits from it. This suggests that expanding access to SAT prep, while a seemingly logical and well-meaning solution, may fall short given the vast lack of accompanying factors that support the effectiveness of SAT prep, namely, universal access to high-quality K–12 education and the influence of social forces that make test prep feel like a normative behavior.

There are two sets of major implications that follow from this. First, inequalities in the benefits derived from test prep undermine the usefulness of SAT scores as a comparison tool between populations, which speaks to how critical holistic admissions review is for recognizing both race and class. It's an awkward subject, but if SAT prep is linked with benefits for one population and not others, it adds some fuzziness to the usefulness of SAT scores as a comparison between students. The idea that admissions officers should "dock" Asian Americans, knowing that they're more likely to receive test prep and actually benefit from it, is ridiculous and unfair. At the same time, though, it raises some questions about whether admissions officers can view and compare scores as "apples to apples." In a system that still insists on using the SAT, these dynamics underscore the need for holistic admissions, which allows admissions officers to gauge accomplishments in the context of opportunity for achievement, which, in turn, is linked to race/ethnicity and social class.

Once again, this doesn't mean that admissions officers should look at a 1550 from an Asian American student and think, "Hmm, well, there's a 50 percent chance that they received coaching. Is it really that impressive?" Rather, this idea—that inequity in both access and benefits associated with SAT prep further justifies the need for (race- and class-conscious) holistic review—is more helpful at the big picture level when you understand that there may be slight discrepancies in the average SAT scores among racial/ethnic groups. To recap the last chapter, these gaps are not particularly large (e.g., thirty to forty points per section at Harvard), but they are hotly contested and used as evidence to argue against race-conscious admissions.

Second, inequalities in the benefits attributed to test prep undermine the effectiveness of the SAT as a barometer for student potential and achievement. Knowing that roughly 40 percent of the East Asian American population, and a good portion of the population of affluent students, will receive test prep makes me wonder, What are we actually measuring here? The SAT folks gave up on trying to claim that they were measuring aptitude or achievement (the mysterious A in SAT) a long time ago and instead just shrugged their shoulders and said, "Hey, it's just a test, we never told you to pay *that* much attention to it." To their credit, they are trying to make the test less coachable—but it will always be coachable, and there will always be certain students who are able to access that coaching more than others. If no one had to use a SAT score for anything—if it could just be treasured private information like your Myers-Briggs personality type—then maybe it would matter less. But admissions offices still take SAT scores seriously—percentiles and ballpark scores are widely advertised—and students look at these to assess "Could I belong here? Should I apply?"

For years, the SAT has attracted criticism for its basic inequity as a test.[30] Even the words appearing on the test may reflect class inequality, such as the use of "oarsman: regatta" as an answer to a question in the analogies section.[31] While this incident happened years ago, it has come to symbolize the inequities that exist within the test—who has a better chance at becoming familiar with it. Naturally, the price of test prep has attracted criticism as well. The College Board has announced efforts to make the test coachable, while somewhat ironically offering coaching resources via Khan Academy.[32] The Khan Academy tutoring, while better than the previous provision of, well, nothing, is well-intentioned, but it reflects the presumption that the biggest issue in SAT prep inequity is the issue of access. It does little to alleviate the tremendous gap in socialization around the test, not to mention the cumulative gap in K–12 equity, which are at the heart of why gaps in SAT achievement persist even when students are given the opportunity to take test prep.[33]

Some might wonder if I'm falling into what George W. Bush called the "soft bigotry of low expectations."[34] My distrust of the SAT is not because I think that low-income populations cannot achieve more with the support of tutoring and extra resources that more affluent students receive regularly. Many can and should. My distrust lies in a test and a system that are structured to reflect existing systemic inequality rather than capture student potential. An excellent example of how the test can fall short is the testimonial of Condoleezza Rice, former provost at Stanford University and US Secretary of State. You may agree or disagree with her politics, but one thing that is undisputed is that Rice is an incredibly smart, disciplined woman (who started college at age sixteen!). In *Extraordinary, Ordinary People: A Memoir of Family* she admitted to having a subpar PSAT score despite excelling overall in school, noting, "My own experience has led me to be rather suspicious of the predictive power of standardized tests."[35] I'm right with you there Condi. My own test scores went up and down a range of 200 or so points, probably depending on the actual content of the test and the test-taking pointers I'd picked up along the way. Did I really get smarter along the way? I doubt it.

What SAT prep really sells is socialization into the test. A high score can be a sign of doggedness and persistence, traits that colleges value, but so are a strong GPA and a challenging course load. SAT prep takes valuable time (and scarce financial resources, for many) away from pursuits that can display mastery and achievement in their own right. For Condi Rice, that was being a star student, accomplished figure skater, and concert pianist. High-achieving students already spend a ridiculous amount of time studying for tests in their regular school setting—is there really a need for yet another one? Test-taking talent, the ability to solve problems in a limited period of time, may be a skill in its own right, whether innate or developed over time. But there's a way to showcase that, too; just make the test optional.

SOME ALTERNATIVES: GOING SAT-OPTIONAL AND AFFIRMING RACE-CONSCIOUS ADMISSIONS

So what are institutions to do? Much evidence works in favor of them going SAT optional, or even canning the SAT altogether. It feels like a scary step, but institutions large and small have gone that way, and the world hasn't crumbled. On the contrary, institutions have raved that going SAT-optional has allowed them to recruit a stronger and more diverse student body.[36] For instance, the president of Hampshire College, Jonathan Lash, writing about his institution's decision to make SAT score submission optional, noted that enrollment of students of color rose 10 percentage points, and the representation of first-generation college students increased from 10 percent to 18 percent.[37] He also reported that the overall quality of the applicants improved: somehow, making the SAT optional, the only major change from previous years, resulted in a more focused applicant pool and gave admissions reviewers a better sense of students' interest in the institution—perhaps because they were less likely to pigeonhole students into an SAT score and more likely to think about their overall merit as a student. Applicant yield, a perennial worry among institutions, rose 8 percentage points from the previous years. What happened at Hampshire College is backed up by research which suggests that dropping the SAT would result in more diverse classes.[38]

Admissions in Texas, under what was originally the Texas 10 Percent Plan, also shows how an admissions process without SAT scores does not result in the student body tanking. The state's 10 Percent Plan is controversial in its overall effectiveness of achieving racial/ethnic diversity.[39] Yet, by and large, it stands as evidence that admissions without SAT scores can result in a talented and highly accomplished class of students. Research on the SAT suggests that the scores themselves are limited in their ability to predict achievement and retention during college.[40] To clarify, the thing they seem to be best at predicting test takers' social class and race/ethnicity. The incongruence between the expected effectiveness of the SAT and the actual, proven limitations certainly makes you wonder. . . .

I've seen this play out firsthand in graduate admissions. Although we have to require GRE scores because of the broader university admissions system, we pay very little actual attention to them. From reviewing the materials provided—the undergraduate transcript, personal statement, resume, and letters of recommendation—we can get a full picture of the applicant's potential to succeed in our rigorous program. Once in a while I'll notice a student with exceptionally high GRE scores and make a mental note that this student might be competitive for one of the university-wide fellowships, which weigh scores heavily. But if the rest of the student's application package does nothing to draw me or the other readers in, the applicant is not considered for further review.

Admissions officers nationwide view SAT-optional as a highly effective strategy, showing that respect for the policy extends even beyond Hampshire College's positive review. The American Council on Education surveyed admissions officers to ask them about the strategies, both race-conscious and race-neutral, that they used in the admissions process. Going SAT-optional was listed as one of the most effective strategies for boosting diversity in the admissions pool.[41] Despite viewing it as highly effective, though, admissions officers reported that few institutions actually made the leap to SAT-optional, reflecting the entrenched status of the test in college admissions.[42] While race-conscious admissions is still greatly needed to ensure both racial and socioeconomic diversity, the legally permissible recognition of race during the admissions process does not preclude using race-neutral approaches to boost diversity, like going SAT-optional. In fact, if there's one race-neutral approach that I can really get behind, it's going SAT-optional. As I've shown, the SAT itself and the concomitant world of SAT prep are heavily racialized and stratified, so going SAT-optional is, in some ways, less a race-neutral strategy and more a strategy that seeks to remove an admissions metric that is unduly shaped by racial and economic inequity.[43]

Findings on the inequities of the SAT and SAT prep also challenge us to reaffirm commitments to race-conscious admissions. The fact that race and class are so strongly correlated with performance on the SAT necessitates policies that allow institutions to identify both the race/ethnicity and social class (versus an admissions process that evaluates SAT scores without this context), as explained by Saul Geiser of the Center for the Study of Higher Education at the University of California, Berkeley. In studying applicants to the UC system from 1994 to 2011, Geiser found that family income, parental education, and race/ethnicity explained over one-third of the variation in SAT scores.[44] He writes: "Race now uniquely accounts for the largest share [of variance in SAT scores]. These findings underscore the continuing relevance of the original, remedial rationale for affirmative action. Rather than a remedy for historical discrimination, however, they show that *race-conscious policies are essential to remedy unwarranted disparities in the present day. The adverse racial impact of SAT scores is far out of proportion with their limited capacity to predict how applicants will perform in college.*"[45]

Geiser does not advocate for a total elimination of the SAT, noting that "scores add a small but statistically significant increment to predictions of college performance."[46] He does, however, contend that given the large association between scores, race, and class, measures like race-conscious admissions are necessary for taking the context of educational inequality into account. Recognizing that standardized tests afford some utility at institutions that receive thousands and thousands of applications, he affirms the simultaneous necessity of being able to consider race in understanding scores: "This is the key point—if the SAT is considered an educational necessity, then consideration of race is also necessary in order to remedy the substantial adverse impact of test scores, beyond what can be reasonably justified by their measurement validity."[47] In other words, this not an either-or scenario; we can simultaneously utilize *both* the SAT *and* race- and class-conscious admissions.

Finally, research on the inequities of SAT prep supports calls for a significant reenvisioning of our admissions system. Harvard law professor Lani Guinier has called out the farce that is our current admissions system, which presents itself as meritocratic and fair in a system that is anything but.[48] Correspondingly, Natasha Warikoo at the Harvard Graduate School of Education has discussed how we live under the illusion that selective admissions really is a selection of the best and brightest, when in reality it is more a winnowing of the elite and those who know how to navigate the system. Even worse, she comments, the system brainwashes its beneficiaries into making them think that they are the truly deserving, the ones who have *earned* their way into the system and not just born on third base.[49]

The answer to inequity is not to go back to a system of standardization, to solely rely on a test score or even a GPA. This is not fairness. Critics of race-conscious admissions gripe that it is unfair to evaluate test scores in the context they come from, seeing it as counterproductive to the entire idea of having *standardized* tests. But what is fairness? Is it fair that so much of a child's life opportunities are shaped by the color of their skin and size of their parent's bank account? Sean Reardon reports that the most affluent and least affluent school districts in America have performance levels that are over four grade levels apart. The racial achievement gap also persists: "On average white students score one and half or more grade levels higher than black and Hispanic students enrolled in socioeconomically similar school districts."[50] I think that most people would agree that these conditions are patently unfair. What choice do children have in where they grow up or what school district they're in? In light of the rampant lack of fairness and inequality that persists in our country, does it make sense to have a one-size-fits-all standardized system?

So what will it take to reimagine a system of admissions that makes educational opportunity not just something for a minority slice of students but for the majority? It obviously needs investments in supporting our K–12 system, which itself is broken. And it will require strengthening existing institutions and creating new, innovative, and excellent ones that are equipped to serve the wide range of students who comprise today's college population. As Saul Geiser reminds us, if the SAT remains, so must race- and class-conscious admissions. And if the SAT goes—which I would be happy to see, making the SAT optional will require both more readers and more time to evaluate applications without the crutch of test scores. It will require the overall strengthening of the diverse institutions that make up US higher education. Why higher education is always so obsessed with scarcity, I do not know. Okay, I do know. Eliteness, that's why. But why must excellence be scarce? It certainly doesn't have to be, but it's often underfunded at places that take a more democratic approach to making excellence accessible—especially at our nation's Historically

Black Colleges and Universities, Tribal Colleges, Hispanic Serving Institutions, Asian American, Native American, and Pacific Islander Serving Institutions, and the like.

It's easy for me to say these things. I'm a researcher; my job is to uncover and highlight the problems. And the SAT is a huge one. It is my dear hope that some of you holding this book are really in the position to enact the radical changes needed to make the system a little better. Don't be distracted by the easy solutions—inequity in admissions won't be solved by offering universal test prep. The system itself needs to first become more sensitive to the rampant inequities that exist and then respond accordingly.

CHAPTER SIX

The Problem of the "Problem of Mismatch"

BEFORE HIS PASSING, Supreme Court Justice Antonin Scalia made headlines during the hearing of *Fisher II v. Texas* when he off-handedly remarked that African American students might do better at "a less-advanced school, a slower-track school where they do well."[1] Talk about an awkward moment; many in the courtroom cringed at both his comment and apparent lack of awareness of why it was so painful.

As offensive as Scalia's comment was, I hear versions of it in (barely) more politically correct forms when people muse about whether URM students are really able to compete at the level of Whites and Asian Americans, or when they remark on how URM students don't really "deserve" to be enrolled at elite institutions and are there only because of affirmative action. Behind Justice Scalia's comment was basically a rephrasing of the mismatch argument, the theory that Black, Latinx, and Native Americans would be better served by attending lower-selectivity institutions because they largely flounder at high-selectivity institutions. Proponents of mismatch argue that race-conscious admissions policies are actually doing URM students a disservice because they underperform at more elite institutions and could better realize their potential in less competitive settings.

So is this true? In this chapter we'll explore the evidence presented by the mismatch folks and investigate whether their theory is substantiated by the actual data. To do this, I'll showcase the work of a lot of smart folks who have been studying this topic for years. Then I'll comment on other ways the discourse on mismatch is deeply flawed due to how it puts the vast onus of responsibility for success or failure on the student instead of the institution. It also largely ignores the ways that majority-status students—White and East Asian Americans—flounder in higher education and the need for the higher education system to improve.

WHY IS THE MISMATCH STEREOTYPE SO POWERFUL?

Before going into the studies that refute mismatch, it's worth considering why the myth of mismatch is so powerful and pervasive—what can research on cognitive bias tell us? When I say that I am challenging mismatch, it's important to consider that, yes, there may be individual cases where students of all race/ethnicities feel that if they had attended a different institution, they would have experienced better outcomes. However, the arguments and political agenda of mismatch advocates go much further to argue that URM students broadly are hurt by attending elite institutions, whether for undergraduate or graduate education. This claim is definitely worth challenging.

Arguably, explicit and implicit stereotypes undergird the grating rhetoric and faulty research around mismatch. Much of it is the sort of patronizing, "benevolent" racism that espouses concern about the well-being of URM students but still reinforces harmful stereotypes. As we will discuss later, proponents of mismatch have misinterpreted statistics or misattributed causality; they identify cause-and-effect relationships that actually cannot be made. Although it is difficult to assess how much of this is influenced by the stereotypes and implicit biases through which people filter information, other cognitive biases can help explain the unfortunate staying power of the theory of mismatch.

One reason why the mismatch stereotype is so powerful is something researchers call *group attribution error*. Basically, this bias happens when people think that the characteristics of an individual are reflective of an entire group. In Ruth Hamill, Richard Nisbett, and Timothy Wilson's groundbreaking study. participants received a narrative about someone who had received welfare: half the group received information stating that the person had been on welfare for a typical length of time, and the other half received information saying that the individual had been on welfare longer than is typical.[2] When surveyed later, *all* the participants had extremely negative views on *all* welfare recipients, showing how information given about an individual had extended to represent the entire group. The negative views persisted regardless of which set of additional information the participant received about the welfare recipient.

What does this have to do with mismatch? The concept of group attribution error helps us understand that people all too easily translate information about an individual into broader assumptions about a group, often without deeply considering whether a sample (or an n of 1) is really representative of a broader population. With mismatch, it seems likely that similar processes are occurring. The book *Mismatch: How Affirmative Action Hurts the Students It's Supposed to Help and Why Universities Won't Admit It*, written by UCLA professor Richard Sander and journalist Stuart Taylor, relies heavily on vignettes about URM students who performed less than ideally at their particular institutions.[3] And while the anecdotes make for persuasive, vivid reading and create a powerful tale when combined with what appears to be solid statistical analyses, a closer look at the data shows that, by and large, the claim that URM students are rampantly mismatched at elite institutions is unsupported.

CHALLENGING MISMATCH

Claims around mismatch were challenged wide scale in 1998 with the publication of *The Shape of the River: Long-Term Consequences of Considering Race in College and University Admissions*, by William Bowen and Howard Bok, former presidents of Princeton University and Harvard University, respectively. *Shape of the River* was one of the first studies to use national datasets to look at what was going on with URM students at elite institutions—were they graduating or slipping behind, as proponents of mismatch would predict? Bok and Bowen's pioneering volume found that URM students had high graduation rates; not only that, those who attended more selective institutions were significantly more likely to graduate and earn advanced degrees—a complete reversal of the theory of mismatch. *Shape of the River* did not claim that complete equity has been achieved. Indeed, Bowen and Bok address head-on the study's finding that on average African American students had lower college GPAs than White students with equivalent social class backgrounds, SAT scores, and high school grades. They noted Claude Steele's work on stereotype threat and the lower availability of URM faculty at elite institutions who can mentor URM students as contributing to the problem.[4] An extensive body of additional research shows how URM students are subject to numerous stressors and hardships during college, which could understandably affect academic performance.[5] Even in the classroom environment, in numerous studies URM students have reported experiencing discrimination and marginalization from faculty as well as peers.[6] Still, these issues are largely the responsibility of the institution or are beyond the immediate control of the student.

Despite the negative conditions that students of color often experience at elite institutions, more recent data indicate that they seem to be doing pretty well, echoing findings from *Shape of the River*. Analyses of nationally representative data by the Georgetown University Center on Education and the Workforce found that graduation rates between White and Black students are fairly even at the top tier of selective institutions: for those with SAT scores in the top half, 85 percent of Black students and 88 percent of White students graduated.[7] For those in the bottom half, 75 percent of White students and 73 percent of Black students graduated. Importantly, the data show that URM students who are especially vulnerable—Latinx and Black students who scored in the bottom quartile of test takers, many of whom are from low-income backgrounds—do notably better in academically challenging environments.

The main takeaway is that students of all races/ethnicities fare much better at more competitive institutions versus open-access institutions, which only graduate 51 percent of students (and 46 percent of URM students), as compared to more selective institutions' graduation rates of 85 percent of their students (and 81 percent of URM students). Study after study affirms that little evidence of mismatch exists at the undergraduate level writ large.

There are a number of things within the selective college environment that help explain the link with higher graduation rates. It is noteworthy that you can take students with similar prior levels of academic achievement, put them in different environments, and reach such different results. More selective institutions tend to have smaller class sizes, more resources for students, more financial aid, and the like. Not only do students in general graduate at higher rates in these institutions, but URM students—the ones who are often assumed to be behind the curve—graduate at high rates as well. As Anthony Carnevale, director of the Georgetown University Center on Education and the Workforce, commented on the report refuting mismatch, "We're holding qualified students back, particularly minorities, saying they can't succeed when in reality, they indeed can."[8]

MISMATCH AND STEM—MOVE THE STUDENT OR CHANGE THE INSTITUTION?

A common question is whether students are staying in the fields that they went to college to pursue, and the mismatch camp argues that URM students would be more likely to persist in certain majors or career paths if they attended less-competitive institutions. An example would be the student who starts out in pre-med with a biology major, does poorly in the intro weed-out courses, and switches to psychology. This scenario happens over and over again, but it becomes especially worrisome if it's weeding out URM talent desperately needed in STEM fields, where the workforce is disproportionately male, White, and East/South Asian American. The scenario of the student starting out in a STEM major and switching out happens over and over again for students of all races. (It felt like 75 percent of my freshman class started out pre-med.)

On top of that, it appears that URM students seem to be thriving in the sciences at some institutions, and less so at others. Places like Xavier University and the University of Maryland, Baltimore County (UMBC), are known for graduating strong cohorts of Black students in the STEM fields. The mismatch folks logically think that these institutions, along with those that are well-regarded but a step below the most competitive (e.g., the Ivy League, UC Berkeley), should be the primary destination for the upper echelon of academically gifted URM students. Let's unpack that idea.

Number 1, places like Xavier and UMBC are in no way "less advanced" or "slower-track" at all. Contrary to Scalia's deficit-laden line of thinking, the reason why URM students are excelling at these institutions isn't because these schools are easy, but because they're providing support to match the rigor of the coursework.

Number 2, URM students succeed at other selective institutions when offered similar levels of support. Take Uri Treisman's calculus initiative at UC Berkeley. Treisman, now at the University of Texas, Austin, started his program out of observations that talented Black students were falling behind in advanced math courses, while Chinese American students were pulling strong grades.[9] An outsider might easily invoke racial stereotypes to assume that one group was simply more intelligent, or more equipped to survive in the "sink or swim" culture of STEM classrooms. However, Treisman examined how the two groups were approaching their studies. He noticed that the Chinese American students made studying almost a social event; they tended to study in groups of friends and spent a lot of time together. When one student got stumped, other students helped them hammer out the solutions. In contrast, Black students tended to study alone for whatever reason—perhaps a holdover from high school, or they had trouble finding study partners in college. Regardless, this technique lent itself to isolation in the face of challenging college curriculum. Ultimately, there was nothing inherently mystical about "Asian intelligence"; nor were the Chinese American students smarter. The real differences pertained to *how* they studied and the relational networks they built to help them navigate challenging coursework. Based on this observation, Treisman devised a program that blended academic and social support, helping URM students form similar study communities that could help them get through challenging coursework. And yes, if you were wondering, the academic performance of the Black and Brown students who participated in the intervention improved notably.

Number 3, the answer to boosting STEM retention isn't to route URMs to lower-tier schools. The problem is that STEM education itself is broken, and not just for URM students. Giant class sizes, the sink-or-swim climate, and lackluster pedagogy are all culprits.[10] But yes, there are issues that especially affect URM students. Studies documenting why URM students and women leave STEM fields—systematic analyses of sizeable samples and not just cherry-picked anecdotes—seldom find that students are floundering academically or in over their heads to such a degree that they leave STEM, either as an undergraduate degree, a graduate program, or even a career. On the contrary, they are responding to the ubiquitous negative climate they encounter. They may be one of few people who look like them in the classroom or may be excluded from the tight-knit study groups that help students survive coursework. Sander and Taylor might say that these dynamics are proof of mismatch, that these URM students would be on more secure footing at a Historically Black College or University or Hispanic Serving Institution. But rather than move students, why not work to improve institutions? Can't we do better?

Not only that, recent research turns conventional wisdom on its head around why STEM faculty aren't a more diverse bunch. Proponents of mismatch would have you think it's due to URM students getting pushed out of STEM fields because they can't hang with the competition. Another common explanation for why the ranks of STEM faculty aren't more diverse is that it's a pipeline issue—there aren't just enough qualified people in the pool, and this is an issue that stretches back to K–12 education. While widening the pool of young people in STEM from an early age is critical, when highly able women and URM students actually get PhDs, they aren't joining the faculty at the same rate as their White and Asian American male peers. In other words, something else is discouraging them from pursuing the faculty route, as shown in a paper published in PLOS ONE by Kenneth Gibbs Jr., John McGready, Jessica Bennett, and Kimberly Griffin.[11] An important critique of the pipeline metaphor is that it's a passive image which suggests that people of color just somehow fall off the ladder (or pipe, I guess) because they can't cut it. In contrast, the work by Gibbs and colleagues shows that it's more like whack-a-mole, where significant structural forces are knocking highly talented folks out of contention. Their study shows that URMs are severely underrepresented in the ranks of STEM faculty not because they are flunking out at the undergraduate level en masse or being mismatched at elite institutions, which leads to getting knocked out of the pipeline. Data from a sample of 1,500 recent PhDs from the biomedical sciences showed that female and URM students were significantly less likely to want faculty careers at the end of their doctoral work than were their White and Asian American male peers, even when career goals, number of publications, support from faculty, research self-efficacy, and graduate training experiences were controlled for. In other words, there's something else that's pushing women and URMs from retaining their interest in faculty careers, and it's not their actual qualifications, accomplishments, interest, or self-confidence. Their study suggests that there are issues during the STEM graduate school process related to the chilly climate in these programs that are largely to blame. The day-to-day psychological wear and tear of isolation experienced by URM students and women affects equity in STEM, even when you have the cream of the crop—students who have made it to the PhD. They suggest a shift in thinking about the underrepresentation of women and URMs as just a pipeline issue (the passive idea that the talent just doesn't get retained along the pathway) to a broader approach that tackles the climate within STEM education.

So yes, there are issues around STEM—but not that URMs are incapable of thriving in the field. Furthermore, URM excellence at Minority Serving Institutions versus traditionally White institutions (TWIs) is not an either-or scenario: both can and should exist. The same institutional reforms that could help URMs and women at TWIs are often the ones that can benefit *all* students in STEM environments. The answer isn't to just move students to different institutions but for institutions writ large to step up their game in improving STEM education for all students, with particular support for underrepresented subgroups. Now let's turn our attention to another idea driving the theory of mismatch: the cascade effect.

THE CASCADE EFFECT AS CULPRIT: RICHARD SANDER'S TAKE

The godfather and leading advocate of mismatch research, Richard Sander, is quick to point out that he believes that URM students are as talented as they come and that he actively supports these students receiving the best education possible. He often highlights his bona fide credentials as someone who has worked in and supported civil rights causes for years. Though his intentions may be good, his interpretation of statistics and approach to statistical analyses are flawed. Interestingly, one of the mantras echoed throughout *Mismatch* is that the book is presenting FACTS, and not just facts but EMPIRICAL FACTS.[12] Nothing else to see here ma'am, just the facts, plain and simple. I have to hand it to him—if I didn't have training in how to conduct and interpret statistical analyses, not to mention the habit of mentally slicing and dicing studies to second-guess whether what is being said is actually supported by the data, then *Mismatch* would be a pretty compelling book. Tag-teaming with journalist Stuart Taylor,

Sander really knows how to pull at your heartstrings. They provide stirring anecdotes of students who feel that they would have succeeded more at other institutions and (seemingly) alarming statistics—Is this not compelling evidence that mismatch is a real thing and that taking away race-conscious admissions will be good for everyone?

Mmm . . . no. In many cases, what Sander and Taylor present as supposedly bulletproof FACTS are more like their *interpretation* of statistics, and where they get in muddy waters is when they throw out assurances of causality—that y exists because of x—with an air of confident certainty. The problem is that often in statistics our ability to prove that an outcome of y is actually caused by x is limited, even by fancy advanced statistical techniques. We can show relationships or linkages but very rarely cause and effect. Generally, this plays out in *Mismatch* when Sander and Taylor present an outcome—for example, gaps in GPAs between URM students and their peers. Then they rush in with an explanation of the cause—it's because of mismatch! In their world, if almost all URMs got bumped down a tier (students attend a California State University institution instead of a University of California one), things would all be better—the racial equity gap would magically close and we'd have Black scientists raining down from the sky.

Okay, maybe that last part is a bit of an exaggeration, but not by much in the odd cause-effect world of mismatch. Sander and Taylor blame something they call the "cascade effect" as a key source of the issue. They argue that because of race-conscious admissions, there's a top tier of URM students who attend the most highly selective and elite institutions who would be better off a tier below. They propose: "The elite schools get their pick of the most academically qualified minorities, most of whom might have been better matched at a lower tier school."[13] And then the big problem happens (according to them, not me), because greater mismatch occurs for each subsequent tier of institution between the average qualifications of majority-status students (which affects the pace of teaching, competitiveness, etc.) and the qualifications of the URM students. And all of this somehow makes the whole operation fall apart for URM students.

Their ideal solution is to have notably fewer URM students in the top-tier institutions—basically only those who would already gain acceptance via an admissions system where the only criteria were SAT scores and GPAs. But, puzzlingly, they recognize that elite institutions "often boast excellent outcomes for their minority students who are, after all, coming in with very impressive credentials."[14] And of course their observation is supported by numerous studies, from the original *Shape of the River* analysis to the more recent study from Georgetown. The real "problems," they say, start at the lower-tier institutions, due to the cascade effect, wherein each tier of institutions gets a class of URM students who are ostensibly less qualified to be there, which has an adverse impact on graduation rates and the like.

But isn't this all evidence of what opponents of mismatch are saying all along, that URM students tend to do better at better-resourced institutions? And if the real problem is at the lower-tier institutions, why is the mismatch debate so obsessed with arguing that URM students are mismatched at *elite* institutions? And why do they make these claims when Sander and Taylor themselves admit that URM students are doing pretty well at top-tier institutions?

These are some of the contradictions of the mismatch argument that I don't really get. Richard Sander, if you're reading this somewhere out there in sunny California, you're probably tearing your hair out reading my take on your (very interesting) book. I agree with you that there is a persistent racial equity gap in standardized measures of academic achievement between URM and White and (many but not all) Asian Americans across institutional tiers. But I disagree that the solution is to just bump the URM students down a tier or two. Because, as Sander and Taylor themselves display in their own book, when given the opportunity in a supportive environment URM students can do great things—even beyond what standardized tests might predict.

As they show in a graphic displaying the percent of Black students receiving STEM degrees at the University of Michigan (for students enrolling in 1999, before Proposal 2 banned consideration of race in the admissions process) a greater percentage of Black students in the top high school academic index earned STEM degrees than did White students—43 percent versus 33 percent.[15] Also in the middle range a greater percentage of Black students earned such degrees, 23 percent compared to 16 percent. And in the bottom tier Black students still outpaced White students in STEM degree attainment, 5 percent to 4 percent. Overall, 22.6 percent of Black students at the University of Michigan earned STEM degrees, compared to 23.1 percent of White students—a negligible difference.[16] Isn't that good news?

But in the world that Sander and Taylor propose, those middle- and bottom-tier Black students would not have the opportunity to attend the flagship University of Michigan campus. In line with the cascade effect theory, if those Black students had attended less-competitive institutions, an even higher percentage with middle- and lower-tier academic indices would have graduated with STEM degrees. However, that speculative outcome is impossible to know, and it appears that when stacked against White students of comparable high school academic indexes, Black students at Michigan earned STEM degrees at higher rates regardless of academic index.

Sander lauds the Cal State system for being an excellent place—and to him, a better fit—for talented URM students. But while the Cal States are doing a great job of supporting URM students, their enrollments are maxed out.[17] I guess his answer would be to knock those students down to the community college level, which seems like an odd solution.

In proposing that we seal off the upper echelons of higher education from a significant percentage of students of color, despite their strong academic performance and real potential, proponents of mismatch are flirting with a troubling type of social engineering, one where opportunities are blocked off to students generally capable of doing the work, and doing the work well. Yes, students should be counseled to help them make informed choices. They should be asked: Would you rather be a big fish in a smaller pond or a little fish in a big pond? What are the learning environments in the various institutions? How might you benefit from the intimacy of a small, liberal arts college experience, or the seemingly limitless number of options present at a large state university? What are the pros/cons to being in an honors college at a state university versus attending an elite private institution? What type of debt might you accrue at various institutions, and how might that affect your ability to pursue graduate education? These are all worthy questions when navigating the jungle of college admissions. But to simply close the doors of elite institutions to high-achieving URM students who could thrive there? That's a totally different and highly problematic proposal.

ARE TEST SCORES AND GPAS THE FULL STORY?

Not only does mismatch research overstate causality, its narrow reliance on standardized academic metrics (usually high school GPA and SAT, or GPA and LSAT score) overlooks factors that influence student success. An established body of work demonstrates that standardized tests do not represent the true potential of URM students; further, standardized academic metrics overlook the other traits that make someone a successful student, or future scientist, lawyer, or doctor.[18] The research on grit is subject to debate.[19] Still, there is something to be said about the type of passion-driven determination that can yield tremendous results but that doesn't always show up on standardized tests, which instead are strongly linked to both race and class.[20]

William Sedlacek has done some of the most extensive research on how universities can use variables beyond standardized academic metrics to capture a diverse and talented class.[21] He found that measures beyond standardized tests and GPAs can help attract a diverse and accomplished talent pool. Similarly, the Posse Foundation is another organization which knows that to capture talent, you have to look beyond test scores. Posse sends cohorts of diverse students to institutions that badly need both diversity and students who can bring leadership to critical issues, the idea being that students in the cohort will help support each other. While students—mostly low-income, people of color, and first generation—have to take the tests and have solid academic records, the competitive selection process looks for additional factors like leadership, passion, and commitment to community to identify accomplishments that aren't fully showcased by test scores.

But this sort of research is generally dismissed by the mismatch camp. Ironically, Sander has got what he wanted—sort of—but he isn't happy. The consideration of race is banned or highly limited in key states like California, Michigan, and to some extent Texas. But it's not enough for him because in his book, he slams both the race-neutral holistic process used by the University of California system as well as the Top 10 Percent Plan used by Texas. He writes that holistic review takes too many factors and contexts into account that depart from the core of GPA and SAT, which he views as the most effective and pure measures of achievement. Texas's system loses for admitting on the basis of class rank. According to him, both result in underqualified students being admitted.[22]

Now, I'm not a huge fan of either system for different reasons (I wish California could consider race, and Texas's process is too rigid), but reading Sander's commentary makes me realize that the world he wants to live in is one that wholly rejects the idea that excellence can come in forms other than a SAT score. It's a philosophical difference, and one that is not insignificant. As an educator, I can say that's not really a world I want to live in.

A Note on Law Schools

The fear of mismatch is not limited to the undergraduate level; a significant part of the controversy over mismatch is around law school admissions. In his dissenting opinion to the 2003 *Grutter v. Bollinger* decision, which affirmed affirmative action, Supreme Court Justice Clarence Thomas (What is it with these Supreme Court Justices?) wrote: "The Law School tantalizes unprepared students with the promise of a University of Michigan degree and all of the opportunities that it offers. These overmatched students take the bait, only to find that they cannot succeed in the cauldron of competition."[23] Seriously dramatic, but is it true?

Sander's studies have found some interesting things. His first study to make a splash in the media found that Black students who took the bar exam passed at a lower rate than Whites.[24] This would certainly seem to be cause for concern, but the social scientist in me asks whether bar passage rates are an adequate measure for settling the huge question of whether places like UCLA, Stanford, and Berkeley should admit fewer URM students or not. The real question is whether the outcomes examined match the actual content of the construct being studied. *Construct validity* is important because you may have a lovely study and find some significant effects, but the outcome of what you're studying may not actually be measuring the construct that you say you are, which is a pretty big problem.

Sander's study spawned a number of critiques of his approach to data analysis and his inappropriate attributions of causality (saying that x causes y, when in reality the methods used are inconclusive). In a reanalysis of Sander's data, Stanford Law School professor Daniel Ho concluded that "correcting the assumptions and testing the hypothesis directly shows that for similarly qualified black students, attending a higher-tier law school has no detectable effect on bar passage rates."[25] His conclusions are in good company: seven other, separate critiques also reanalyzed Sander's data and challenged his conclusions as being unsupported by the data.[26] Elsewhere, Sander claimed that the bar passage rate for Black test-takers from the University of Michigan Law School was 62 percent on the first attempt and only 76 percent after multiple takes, a worrisome trend.[27] However, when replicating the analysis using data from the most selective law schools in Michigan, Richard Lempert, Eric Stein Distinguished University Professor of Law and Sociology, Emeritus, at the University of

Michigan, found that 78 percent of African American test-takers passed on the first attempt and 90.9 percent passed with multiple takes—much higher numbers.[28]

Of course one would hope to see total 100 percent bar passage from all groups, but law schools generally give little space to actually teach the content that makes up the majority of the bar exam. This doesn't mean that URM students are performing poorly writ large in law school and thus need to be at less-rigorous institutions but that they may not be doing as well at an exam that surprise surprise, law school does little to actually prepare you for. Additionally, not passing the bar initially doesn't doom your legal career. It's not ideal, but there are second chances. Not only that, but there is a distinguished lineage of individuals who have failed the bar at least once and seem to be doing just fine. US Senator and former California attorney general Kamala Harris has been open about not passing the bar the first time around, and she seems to be doing pretty well. I continue to be amazed that Hillary Clinton failed the DC bar, mainly because the idea of Hillary Clinton not excelling in any academic scenario is unfathomable—but it's true! And Kathleen Sullivan, the former Harvard Law professor and dean of Stanford Law, flunked the California bar the first time around, even with years of experience in the legal profession. I'm guessing that no one suggested that she should have gone to a "slower track" institution.

Even though plenty of White folks seem to be flunking the bar (JFK Jr. anyone?), there's no questioning their collective presence at America's top law schools. Instead, we're reminded again and again that the California or DC exams are notoriously hard. But when URM students fail? Well, they just can't cut it in the "cauldron of competition." (I hope you can tell I'm being sarcastic.) For additional summary and critique of Sander's work, I suggest the friend of the court brief filed by Richard Lempert in *Fisher II v. University of Texas, Austin*, which provides commentary on a number of key studies informing the mismatch debate.[29] Now, back to the undergrads.

DON'T BLAME THE STUDENT. CHANGE THE INSTITUTION

Often missing from the mismatch debate is the idea that institutions need to step up and recognition of the challenges encountered by non-URM students. We know from the research that even students who come in with SAT scores below the mean graduate at notably higher rates from selective institutions versus open-access institutions.[30] They can do the work. The decision to leave an institution or change a major is deeply complex and is seldom an issue of academics alone. There are financial pressures, life circumstances, and students juggling work and school. And then there are issues of climate—Do URM students have the ability to experience role modeling and mentoring? Are URM students included in study groups? Do they get the privilege of not having to worry about minute or more pronounced instances of racial discrimination from fellow students or even faculty? Do they have the support to participate in all of the "extras," such as an undergraduate research experience, internship, and the like? Research suggests that the answer to these questions is generally "no."[31] There is a lot of room for institutions to improve how they approach undergraduate education, and the solution is not to radically re-sort URM students into lower-tier schools, but instead to see how all institutions can better support student success, especially for those who have been historically disenfranchised.

Additionally, the rhetoric linked to mismatch is deeply problematic because it puts the onus of responsibility for success or failure on the student and the student alone, instead of presenting it as something that is also shared by the institution. Work by Estela Bensimon from the University of Southern California's Center for Urban Education has uncovered how educators are commonly affected by this damaging rhetoric and how they carry stereotypes and low expectations into their work with URM students, which in turn creates a negative feedback loop where students are not well-supported.[32] It's not that individual responsibility and initiative are irrelevant, but there are entrenched structural forces that influence how different students experience higher education.

Sander might agree that institutions matter—but then he would say that the solution is to send these URM students to friendlier (or, as Scalia would say, "slower-track") institutions. Never mind that they are already graduating at basically the same rates as other students at more selective institutions. Higher education can and should do better, and it's not just that URM students need a great education; a great education needs URM students.

DON'T FORGET WHITE AND ASIAN AMERICANS . . . BUT WE DO

Personal story time. When I moved to Los Angeles for graduate school, I started meeting Asian American guys who had not yet finished college at UCLA or were back in school in their late twenties/early thirties to finish off a degree they'd started years earlier. Their stories shared a general theme of how they had floundered academically during some period and had to leave. There were usually stints with academic probation mixed in. Most eventually finished—some at UCLA, others elsewhere—but it took a while, and their paths definitely departed from the traditional four- to five-year course of undergraduate education, let alone from the stereotype of Asian Americans being academically successful.

When I think back, I know that they *all* struggled with their own cultural baggage, mainly the stigma that Asian Americans aren't supposed to fail. Many of them avoided telling their parents for years. But no one ever suggested that they were mismatched—that was a type of stigma that they never had to deal with. Their individual failures were all personal and compounded by the stereotype that they weren't supposed to fail—but they never had to carry the heavy burden of feeling that their failure was actually confirming a stereotype.

While retention for Asian Americans is, on average, higher than it is for URM groups, disaggregating by ethnicity tells a different story. Data from the UC Davis incoming 1998 freshman class indicate that while 87.7 percent of Chinese American students graduated in six years, only 66 percent of Korean American and 71.7 percent of Vietnamese American students did.[33] In comparison, 74.7 percent of African American students graduated within six years. Even though graduation rates for both Korean and Vietnamese American students were lower than those for African American students, I've never heard any sweeping rhetoric related to these Asian American students which suggests that they need to be at "slower-track" institutions. Hey, they're the model minority! And yet they too need our help, since they also easily slip through the cracks.

I'm not saying that (East and South) Asian Americans and White students are the only ones who really need our attention, but I highlight these statistics to show that sizeable numbers of students struggle, and it's not just URM students. Majority-status students have the privilege of struggling without the sweeping label of mismatch, but students of all races are still not being retained. Simply put, US higher education can do better for all students. In a system where only 33 percent of the people in our country complete a four-year degree, it's not an issue of individuals being mismatched but of a whole system that needs critical attention.[34] Using mismatch theory to justify the serious reduction of URM students being admitted to selective universities falls short in addressing who actually might be struggling in college. Furthermore, universities would be better served to focus attention on vulnerable students and students who indicate that they are struggling at critical junctures—which may include URM students but also cuts across to first-generation students, low-income students, and any student who's in in over their head.

ANECDOTES, VIGNETTES, AND THE LIMITATIONS OF MISMATCH "THEORY"

Mismatch is replete with compelling anecdotes of students who think they would have done better at another institution. Even the reader reviews on the book's Amazon.com page are replete with people feeling like Sander and Taylor are telling their story too. But saying "I've heard this a lot" or "This happened to me" on its own doesn't constitute good research; we need to look at the data. And the data show that by and large, URM students are succeeding at top-tier institutions and overall are doing better at academically stronger institutions.[35] Yes, there are always students (of all races) who fall through the cracks, but why this happens is a much more complex story than the one proposed by Sander and Taylor, and it isn't fixed by summarily bumping everyone down a tier—that's the real mismatch going on.

But if the data don't convince you, we can look to some of Sander and Taylor's words that make a little more sense to me. I'll give it to him—for someone whose book repeatedly slams race-conscious policies and has filed multiple amicus (friend of the court) briefs lobbying for an end to race-conscious admissions, Richard Sander is a man of some surprises. Despite dedicating its pages to talking about how the world is melting because of race-conscious admissions (not to mention part of the title being *How Affirmative Action Hurts the Students It's Supposed to Help*), in its conclusion *Mismatch* doesn't fully advocate for ending race-conscious admissions.[36] They themselves state in the concluding pages of their book:

> Most or all of the black and Hispanic students admitted to these top schools are so smart and able that a substantial minority might be admitted without preferences, and the rest with preferences smaller than those that less elite schools use. In addition, the institutional resources to help any struggling students succeed are abundant. Another advantage is that preferentially admitted students at these top schools will get to know many classmates who will be future leaders. After graduation, the reputational and networking benefits of a super-elite degree are in some ways unique. So all graduates of

> these very top institutions have good odds of finding niches where they will thrive.[37]

Why yes Richard Sander, I agree. Top schools definitely need "smart and able" URM students, so let's leave it at that.

CHAPTER SEVEN

How Then Should We Think?

A Conclusion

WELL, WE'VE GONE through quite a bit. From challenging class-based affirmative action and mismatch to realizing that Black kids aren't always stuck in the cafeteria together, hopefully you're better equipped to distinguish between the hype versus the actual research on how diversity works in higher education. So moving forward, how then should we think? A few recommendations to consider.

THE POWER OF COGNITIVE BIAS

Writing this book was a humbling experience for me because I was constantly reminded of my own blind spots when it comes to understanding admissions and campus climate, except it's a little more embarrassing for me since I study this stuff full time. I still recall the moment I realized that I had totally missed Espenshade and Radford's finding that significant preferences are given to *low-income* students of color, including Asian Americans. Or the surprise I felt when I stumbled on Reardon and colleagues' counterintuitive finding that institutions can actually get to more economic diversity when they consider *both* race and class in the admissions process, instead of focusing on class alone. And I, too, used to be on the bandwagon that if we just expanded SAT prep to everyone, we'd take care of the bulk of our equity issues around standardized testing.

But does understanding some of the processes behind the why and how of why we miss critical information when it is right there in front of us (enter gorilla on the basketball court) necessarily mean that we will rethink our assumptions? Truth be told, I'm not sure. In fact, a disturbing amount of research signals that we are incapable of changing our minds, even when confronted with disconfirming evidence. Psychologists have identified the *continued influence effect*, which shows that we're quite good at holding on to misinformation, even when corrected.[1] I want to believe that data make a difference; but to play devil's advocate, one could say that research which surprises or challenges our assumptions "sticks" more when it aligns with some broader framework of belief that we already carry—confirmation bias at work. For instance, while I was surprised to find out that under current race-conscious policies low-income and working-class Asian Americans receive a significant leg up in the admissions process, I see how that evidence fits into my broader understanding that race-conscious admissions is generally a good thing—imperfect, but a necessary tool in a larger toolkit that institutions desperately need in order to advance equity. Before you question my credibility, I remind you that you can't make up data, unless you're just a liar or into fake news. You can come up with bad interpretations, but you cannot, or at least should not, just make it up out of thin air. Pull out your copy of Espenshade and Radford, and the finding on low-income Asian Americans is right there on page 98 in plain sight. But *why* does that factoid stick in my brain now? Well, that's the tricky work of cognition and why we gravitate toward some facts—and interpretations of those facts—more than others. I've presented facts, but a lot of what you decide to do with them will probably depend on your own worldview and lens of interpretation. Having a stronger understanding of the pervasiveness of cognitive biases—how we totally rely more on the intuitive and impulsive System 1 instead of the more deliberate and nuanced System 2—and seeing some concrete examples of how it plays out in our real-life thinking on race and diversity in higher education will, I hope, humble us a little. To be a little more skeptical of interpretations of data instead of taking them immediately at face value, to weigh disconfirming evidence, and to not settle for solutions that are easy to understand but fall short of addressing the roots of the problem—these are good steps to take. I am hopeful that if presented with key evidence that any of the claims I've made in this book are wrong, I would be open to changing my mind.

Happily, research on the continued influence effect suggests that while misunderstanding persists when misinformation is simply negated or a quick correction is thrown out, some of the negative effects are reduced when a "plausible causal alternative" is offered. As Hollyn M. Johnson and Colleen M. Seifert of the University of Michigan explain, "Findings suggest that misinformation can still influence inferences one generates after a correction has occurred; however, providing an alternative that replaces the causal structure it affords can reduce the effects of misinformation."[2] It is not as quick and easy as thinking that good data will immediately change everyone's minds, but this is still good news that can make the world a little less terrible, one empirically supported explanation at a time.

AFFIRMING THE ESSENTIALNESS OF RACE-CONSCIOUS ADMISSIONS

It is no secret that the data affirm the use of race in the college admissions process, not just to support racial diversity but also to support economic diversity.[3] It is critical that we reject claims that we have "enough" diversity in higher education when the data indicate that there are serious shortfalls throughout the country. For instance, by googling the racial/ethnic breakdown at UC San Diego, I found a document on the university's website that proudly states: "The undergraduate student body at UCSD is ethnically diverse; approximately 71% of undergraduates are students of color."[4] But when you scroll to the right, you see that African American enrollment in 2016 was 2 percent.[5] So in the UC system the campuses are viewed as highly diverse—after all, Whites are a technical minority—yet only 2 percent of students at UCSD, 2 percent of students at UC Irvine, and 2.5 percent of students at UC Berkeley were Black in recent years.[6]

Further, URM enrollments have not kept up with the explosive growth in the eligible K–12 population in many states. At the University of Texas, Austin, in 2016, 20 percent of undergraduates were Latinx and 3.8 percent were African American.[7] Twenty percent seems like a lot until you realize that, in 2015, 48.5 percent of Texas's public high school seniors were Latinx and 12.6 percent were African American.[8] There may be some improvement in URM enrollments when you compare statistics from years past, but given the explosive demographic growth of students of color in many states, we are not seeing the parallel growth in college enrollments.

These data illustrate the critical need to consider race in the admissions process. Contrary to popular belief, addressing race does not mean admitting someone only because of their race, or even tipping the scale due to race. It is simply being able to know who a student is—a deeper understanding of their context for educational opportunity and what they may bring to the student body. It is about looking at the whole student, not just test scores and GPAs. And yes, when given a chance, the vast majority of these students thrive. Forget the weak claims of mismatch. The real story is so much richer.

THE MEANING OF MERIT

Altogether, what we've discussed on Asian American students, the inequities of SAT prep, and mismatch should give us serious pause when we're thinking about when we say "merit." While narrow conceptions of merit are defined largely by numbers on a scale—SATs and GPAs—we know that college admissions at selective institutions operates in a more holistic fashion, looking at both nonstandardized traits (e.g., essays, leadership, key experiences) and the context surrounding those standardized metrics. So if the SAT average at a particular institution is a bit higher for Asian Americans, as Espenshade himself has said, that's not "smoking gun" evidence of deep-rooted discrimination against Asian Americans. This is a statement I echo, as an Asian American deeply concerned with fair and equitable treatment for my community and family. Operating out of pure self-interest, I want other Asian Americans—especially my own child, who was born during the writing of this book—to go to college where not everyone is admitted just because they have the top test scores or were the valedictorian.[9] I aspire for students to know that excellence comes in many different packages, shapes, colors, and sizes.

It is also critical to recognize that some level of excellence can be bought—at least for certain populations, to put it crudely. And in turn, the research on SAT prep is hard to swallow. On one hand, students can be affirmed for investing the time and discipline to improving their scores through rigorous test prep. On the other hand, not only are there vast inequities in who is able to access high-quality test prep, but the research shows that certain groups—Asian Americans, high-income students, and those who are already high academic achievers—benefit more from test prep than their peers of other race/ethnicities and economic situations.[10] This reality requires a big shift in thinking, from believing that if everyone just had access to the same opportunity that everything would be fair, to realizing that inequality is much more complex than that, and a summer of intensive test prep can't make up for the deeper inequities in K–12 education. It would be one thing if students whose test scores are somewhere below the mean or median completely flounder in higher education, but we know that when given the chance, many of these students can and do succeed. When we reexamine our definitions of merit—not to compromise but to expand the umbrella of who is worthy to experience a well-resourced college education—we all win.

WHAT STUDENTS OF COLOR ARE DOING WHEN THEY'RE NOT IN THE CAFETERIA

If you've made it this far, hopefully you get it: students of color don't camp out all day in the cafeteria with each other. Of course, there are times when they hang out, and we know that that isn't such a bad thing because participation in same-race communities like ethnic student organizations is linked with higher levels of interacting across race. Students of color need time to refuel, and there can be something life affirming (or less ego depleting) about interacting with one's own racial/ethnic group.

But that doesn't mean that students only stay there. The time in ethnic student organizations and other communities helps keep them going when it comes to interacting with the broader diversity of the campus. The key is to make sure that students have plenty of opportunities to engage both across and within racial/ethnic lines. Campuses can create a more fluid and welcoming environment for cross-racial interactions by encouraging socioeconomic diversity within racial/ethnic groups: breaking down the consolidation of privilege and making sure that racial lines aren't reinforced by economic divides.

Also, campuses need to keep a close eye on environments that may shield White students from engaging with the broader diversity of the campus. Greek life needs to be brought into the twenty-first century and be asked difficult questions about the culture it fosters and the types of values, experiences, and friendships of its members. In many cases, the best thing may be to end campus sponsorship of historically White Greek-life organizations.

THE WORK IS FAR FROM DONE

I recently saw a headline in the *Washington Post* for an op-ed written by the dean of Harvard Business School, Nitin Nohria: "We've Gotten Better at Diversity: Now the Challenge Is Inclusion."[11] I guess most institutions only had room for improvement when it came to diversity, so it's not inaccurate (hopefully) to say that we're a bit "better" on that front. Actually, even that statement is refutable, depending on who you ask. But to say that "now the challenge is inclusion" makes it sound like the recruitment and retention of a racially and socioeconomically diverse student body isn't a challenge anymore and that inclusion is the real challenge at hand. That inclusion—more or less, helping people of different backgrounds feel included—is even relevant is a shockingly new idea to a lot of people, so perhaps relative to good ol' been-around-the-block diversity, it is the real challenge.

The growing emphasis on inclusion is critically important, and giving it its own space in the world of diversity conversations is helpful since people tend to focus on composition and enrollment figures when they refer to diversity, even though true diversity has always been about more than numbers. Still, the idea that diversity, even in just the compositional sense, has been "achieved" falls short. We simply haven't achieved compositional diversity in many contexts. Its status is all-too-fragile, and the legality of race-conscious admissions as upheld by Supreme Court rulings might be overturned by the time this book hits the shelves. Additionally, diversity and inclusion are interdependent, symbiotic concepts: you can't have one without the other. Finally, the idea that we've ever "achieved" diversity is a little preposterous. Diversity is an ever-changing and ever-shifting entity, even on the same campus. Even campuses that were once exemplars for diversity can lose ground.[12]

All of this is to say, the idea that diversity is an arc of linear progress (Step 1, recruit diverse student body; Step 2, recruit diverse faculty; Step 3, fix the administration; Step 4, mix it all together and bake in an oven at 475 to reach inclusion) is a façade. That is not to say that everything is hopeless and failing, but the assumption that we've "made it" is anything but. I sit here writing this during a period of what is considered to be the biggest revival of campus activism since the 1960s. My own beloved campus, the University of Maryland, College Park, is an example of a campus that has achieved much in many respects.[13] We have a compositionally diverse student body at the surface level. Many of our hallmark programs are supposed to support a positive campus climate (and some were even pioneered here): intergroup dialogue, cultural competency requirements in general education, fantastic offices like Multicultural Involvement and Community Advocacy and the Office of Diversity and Inclusion, multiple ethnic studies programs and course offerings, a chief diversity officer, etc. And yet, in the past year or so, the alt right movement somehow felt it was their place to plaster the campus with deeply racist and anti-immigrant fliers. A noose was found at one of the historically White fraternities. And it all came to a head commencement weekend 2017, when a visiting African American student from Bowie State University, Lt. Richard Collins III, was brutally murdered by a White University of Maryland student who was later found to have joined an alt right Facebook group. It was a shattering and deeply painful way to end a year that had already been so difficult.

So my campus, yes. Diverse and wonderful in many respects, but when you look beyond the surface less so. Those ethnic studies programs? They're perpetually underfunded. Those cultural competency classes? Most are taught by non-tenure-track lecturers whose employment status is often fragile and continually uncertain. The racially diverse student body? It's definitely an underrepresentation of different ethnic subgroups and low-income students, and the institution could stand to pay a little less attention to the SAT, in my opinion. And sometimes the ugliness is right there at the surface, starkly unavoidable. The fliers, the noose, the killing. I can't believe I'm even writing these words.

I point out all of these things not to say that my campus is a terrible place. There are few places where I'd rather teach. Being the eternal optimist that I am, I believe that tremendous progress and resistance coexist in the face of the brokenness. I highlight these things to show how "diversity" is not a place, state, or status that is reached but an ideal that we continuously and endlessly work toward. It's a component of a broader landscape of justice and equity—not the end goal in and of itself but a means necessary to bring about a better end. Most of all, any sort of superficial diversity that is achieved without a broader and deeper commitment to justice and the eradication of inequality is just window dressing.[14]

I always thought that *inclusion* was a funny word. But now it seems to be the one that encapsulates what people mean when they refer to an ambiguous mix of equity, a sense of belonging, and the actual feeling of being included. It is a laudable thing to shoot for, and the opposite state of exclusion is certainly something that no one wants to have their institution or organization be characterized by. I am all for inclusion. My qualm, though, is when conversations about inclusion promote the assumption, implicit or explicit, that we've checked "diversity" off the to-do list and now can shift gears to "inclusion." In reality, to be engaged in diversity work is to be continuously reminded that racism and challenges to diversity and inclusion are constant issues, not ones that are dealt with through one spectacular initiative or campaign. Diversity and inclusion are inseparable symbiotic concepts that require careful attention, maintenance, and proactive initiative.[15]

ANTIRACISM: WELCOMING BACK THE REASON FOR DIVERSITY

Like diversity, the term *inclusion* can mean too many things to too many people.[16] So along with *diversity* and *inclusion* (or *diversity*, *inclusion*, and *equity*), I suggest the companion *antiracism*. For some time, the term *antiracism* has felt too obvious and over-the-top, almost unnecessary in its directness. Like duh, of course everyone is against racism. In the academy, it has felt like much of the racism was subtle, difficult to put your finger on but there, like the lingering aroma of secondhand smoke. It has meant moments of people of color questioning whether the incident that just happened to them was about race, or their own paranoia. It encompasses the underhanded comments, intentional or not, of good-hearted people saying things like "but there are so few people of color qualified for this type of position" when you're wondering why none of the names you forwarded became actual candidates for the job. Racism is still all of those things—and yes, it's still most difficult to tackle when it's in its subtlest forms and perpetuated by some of the nicest people you'd ever know.

But a funny thing happened around 2014 and beyond that coincided with the chaotic 2016 presidential election and the emergence of movements like Black Lives Matter and the resurgence of campus activism. The stronger, more public presence of overt racism—the alt right, Charlottesville, the endless Facebook feeds showing police brutality, the movements of students of color giving voice to the ugly that they had experienced in higher education—reopened conversations around race and racism that have been awkward and difficult, simultaneously progressive and regressive. In some ways, it feels like we're going backward, because so many (but not all) people can point a finger at White supremacists and feel sanctimonious that they themselves aren't "that horrible," when in fact we all carry part of the disease of America's original sin. But in other ways the developments are helpful when they can nudge people toward an understanding that the eradication of racism is not a linear tale of progress but an ever-present, endemic component of American life, as the critical race theorists say.

Racism and racial inequality are things that we will always have, and with that antiracism—identifying the ugly and working to combat it—must also be a permanent fixture of higher education, like our so-called commitments to diversity and inclusion. Recognizing that racial inequality is a fundamental, ingrained component of higher education is not an admission of hopelessness, of throwing up our arms and saying, "What can we do?" Rather, it marks an honest recognition of the reality that exists and is a call to address it to the best of our ability, which always demands more than the status quo. We may never get "there," but that's not necessarily the worst news. Higher education may be the patient who's on blood pressure medication for the rest of their life; in both cases—higher education and one's health—ignorance is not bliss but a death sentence.[17] But on the matter of racism and racial inequality in higher education, we've been given an opportunity, and not a sentence: to get better, think better, be better, and do better.

IN CLOSING

From the admissions process to where students sit in the cafeteria, race permeates practically every inch of collegiate life—even the spaces that don't explicitly acknowledge it. This book aims to give you some useful tools for deconstructing the commonplace, but often misinformed, assumptions about how race affects how students get to college and what happens to them once they're there. From falsely assuming that SAT scores should determine acceptance to overlooking White students' self-segregation, higher education abounds with situations that are too easily misunderstood at face value.

So maybe that's a final word of endorsement for why diversity matters in colleges and universities: part of getting to a place where we have more just and equitable institutions requires having different types of people, especially those whose voices are historically silenced and persistently underrepresented, to help us see our blind spots and come to a deeper and more complex understanding of the world around us. This is not a diversity that claims to exist for the sake of existing or just to make us feel better about ourselves ("Yay diversity! Everyone is different!") but a diversity that constantly reminds us that our past—when so many people were not allowed to sit at the table—is not behind us but persistently permeates our present.

It's not a call to defensiveness, where we feel like we're beyond "those issues," but a call to recognizing that there is so much that we do not know—and we can only get closer to a fuller understanding by actively courting what has been missing for far too long.

Notes

INTRODUCTION

1. Charles Evain, "Diversity Among the Statistics: Self-Segregation Among Student Groups," *Georgetown Voice*, January 28, 2016, http://georgetownvoice.com/2016/01/28/diversity-beyond-the-statistics-self-segregation-among-student-groups/.
2. Julie J. Park, "Clubs and the Campus Racial Climate: Student Organizations and Interracial Friendship in College," *Journal of College Student Development* 55, no. 7 (2014): 650, doi:10.1353/csd.2014.0076.
3. Nicholas A. Bowman and Julie J. Park, "Interracial Contact on College Campuses: Comparing and Contrasting Predictors of Cross-Racial Interaction and Interracial Friendship," *Journal of Higher Education* 85, no. 5 (2014): 676–78, doi:10.1080/00221546.2014.11777344.
4. Amos Tversky and Daniel Kahneman, "Availability: A Heuristic for Judging Frequency and Probability," *Cognitive Psychology* 5 (1973): 207–32.
5. Daniel Kahneman, *Thinking, Fast and Slow* (New York: Farrar, Straus & Giroux, 2011).
6. With homage to Chimamanda Adichie's TED Talk, "The Danger of a Single Story," featured at https://ed.ted.com/featured/TXtMhXIA.
7. Richard D. Kahlenberg, *The Remedy: Class, Race, and Affirmative Action* (New York: Basic Books, 1996).
8. Soo-yong Byun and Hyunjoon Park, "The Academic Success of East Asian American Youth: The Role of Shadow Education," *Sociology of Education* 85, no. 1 (2012): 54–55, doi:10.1177/0038040711417009; Julie J. Park and Ann H. Becks, "Who Benefits from SAT Prep? An Examination of High School Context and Race/Ethnicity," *Review of Higher Education* 39, no. 1 (2015): 14, doi:10.1353/rhe.2015.0038.
9. Malcolm Gladwell, *David and Goliath: Underdogs, Misfits, and the Art of Battling Giants* (New York: Little, Brown, 2013); Richard Sander and Stuart Taylor Jr., *Mismatch: How Affirmative Action Hurts Students It's Intended to Help, and Why Universities Won't Admit It* (New York: Basic Books, 2012).
10. Sander and Taylor, *Mismatch*.

CHAPTER 1

1. *Mean Girls*, dir. Tina Fey (Los Angeles: Paramount Home Entertainment, 2004), DVD.
2. Beverly D. Tatum, *Why Are All the Black Kids Sitting Together in the Cafeteria? And Other Conversations about Race* (New York: Basic Books, 1997).
3. Berber Jin, "Stanford's Silent Segregation," *Stanford Review*, May 19, 2017, https://stanfordreview.org/stanfords-silent-segregation-35c474f7e7ee; Seth P. Trees, "UF Promoting Racism with New Self-Segregated Housing," *Daily Nerv*, May 22, 2017, https://thedailynerv.com/uf-set-to-open-self-segregated-housing-80fc37feea9d; Catherine Green, "What to Do About Self-Segregation on Campus," *The Atlantic*, December 4, 2015, 3. https://www.theatlantic.com/notes/2015/12/what-do-we-do-about-self-segregation-on-campus-contd/418425/.
4. Nicholas A. Bowman and Julie J. Park, "Interracial Contact on College Campuses: Comparing and Contrasting Predictors of Cross-Racial Interaction and Interracial Friendship," *Journal of Higher Education* 85, no. 5 (2014): 676–78, doi:10.1080/00221546.2014.11777344; Julie J. Park, Nida Denson, and Nicholas A. Bowman, "Does Socioeconomic Diversity Make a Difference? Examining the Effects of Racial and Socioeconomic Diversity on the Campus Climate for Diversity," *American Educational Research Journal* 50, no. 3 (2013): 482.
5. Julie J. Park, "Clubs and the Campus Racial Climate: Student Organizations and Interracial Friendship in College," *Journal of College Student Development* 55, no. 7 (2014): 650, doi:10.1353/csd.2014.0076.
6. Amos Tversky and Daniel Kahneman, "Availability: A Heuristic for Judging Frequency and Probability," *Cognitive Psychology* 5 (1973): 207–32.
7. Veronica Rocha, "Group of Black Women Kicked Off Train in Napa for Laughing Too Loud," *Los Angeles Times*, August 24, 2015, http://www.latimes.com/local/lanow/la-me-ln-black-women-kicked-off-napa-wine-train-20150824-html-story.html.
8. It was even apparent in *Mean Girls*, where it went without saying that the tables of Jocks, Band Geeks, and Plastics were all White.
9. Bowman and Park, "Interracial Contact on College Campuses"; Mitchell J. Chang, Alexander Astin, and Dongbin Kim, "Cross-Racial Interaction Among Undergraduates: Some Causes and Consequences," *Research in Higher Education* 45, 5 (2004): 527–51; Park, Denson, and Bowman, "Does Socioeconomic Diversity Make a Difference?"; Julie J. Park and Young K. Kim, "Interracial Friendship, Structural Diversity, and Peer Groups: Patterns in Greek, Religious, and Ethnic Student Organizations," *Review of Higher Education* 37, no. 1 (2013): 1–24; Victor B. Saenz, "Breaking the Segregation Cycle: Examining Students' Pre-College Racial Environments and College Diversity Experiences," *Review of Higher Education* 34, no. 1 (2010): 17–19.
10. I elaborate on this more in my first book, where I tell the story of a campus religious group with positive intentions toward cultivating racial diversity in

its membership that eventually ran up against the limitations and inequities of a campus that had lost much of its diversity due to a statewide affirmative action ban. See Julie J. Park, *When Diversity Drops: Race, Religion, and Affirmative Action in Higher Education* (New Brunswick, NJ: Rutgers University Press, 2013).

11. Ibid., 128.
12. Anthony L. Antonio, "Diversity and the Influence of Friendship Groups in College," *Review of Higher Education* 25, no. 1 (2001), 79; Victor B. Saenz, Hoi Ning Ngai, and Sylvia Hurtado, "Factors Influencing Positive Interactions Across Race for African American, Asian American, Latino, and White College Students," *Research in Higher Education* 48, no. 1 (2007): 25–34, doi:10.1007/s11162-006-9026-3.
13. James Sidanius, Colette Van Laar, Shana Levin, and Stacey Sinclair, "Ethnic Enclaves and the Dynamics of Social Identity on the College Campus: The Good, the Bad, and the Ugly," *Journal of Personality and Social Psychology* 87, no. 1 (2004): 105, doi:10.1037/0022-3514.87.1.96.
14. Jeff DeSimone, "Fraternity Membership and Binge Drinking" (Working Paper 12468, National Bureau of Economic Research, Cambridge, MA, August 2006), 1–41, http://www.nber.org/papers/w12468; Sidanius et al., "Ethnic Enclaves," 105; Park and Kim, "Interracial Friendship, Structural Diversity, and Peer Groups," *Review of Higher Education* 37, no. 1 (2013): 12–13.
15. Park, *When Diversity Drops*, 19–21; Edgar H. Schein, "Organizational Culture," *American Psychologist* 45, no. 2 (1990): 109–19; Edgar H. Schein, *Organizational Culture and Leadership* (San Francisco: Jossey-Bass, 2004).
16. Huffman, "Campus Racism"; "Self-Segregation Alive and Well on the OU Campus," *The Athens News*, February 12, 2012, https://www.athensnews.com/news/campus/self-segregation-alive-and-well-on-the-ou-campus/article_f45b7154-8fd0-5121-8404-186716907c34.html; Charles Evain, "Diversity Beyond the Statistics: Self-Segration Among Student Groups," Carrying On: A Rotating Column by Voice Staffers, *The Georgetown Voice*, January 28, 2016, http://georgetownvoice.com/2016/01/28/diversity-beyond-the-statistics-self-segregation-among-student-groups/.
17. Anthony DePalma, "Separate Ethnic Worlds Grow on Campus," *New York Times*, May 18, 1991, http://www.nytimes.com/1991/05/18/us/separate-ethnic-worlds-grow-on-campus.html?pagewanted=all.
18. Bowman and Park, "Interracial Contact on College Campuses," 676–78.
19. Park "Clubs and the Campus Racial Climate"; Elizabeth Stearns, Claudia Buchmann, and Kara Bonneau, "Interracial Friendships in the Transition to College: Do Birds of a Feather Flock Together Once they Leave the Nest?" *Sociology of Education* 82, no. 2 (2009): 173–95.
20. Park and Kim, "Interracial Friendship," 12–21.
21. Young K. Kim, Julie J. Park, and Katie Koo, "Testing Self-Segregation: Multiple-Group Structural Modeling of College Students' Interracial Friendship by

Race," *Research in Higher Education* 56, no. 1 (2015): 73–74.

22. N. A. Bowman and J. J. Park, "Not All Diversity Interactions Are Created Equal: Cross-Racial Interaction, Close Interracial Friendship, and College Student Outcomes," *Research in Higher Education* 56, no. 6 (2015): 601–21.
23. Patricia Gurin, Eric L. Dey, Sylvia Hurtado, and Gerald Gurin, "Diversity and Higher Education: Theory and Impact on Educational Outcomes," *Harvard Educational Review* 72, no. 3 (2002): 330–67, doi:10.17763/haer.72.3.01151786u134n051.
24. See Robert Teranishi, *The Relevance of Asian Americans and Pacific Islander in the College Completion Agenda* (New York: National Commission on Asian American and Pacific Islander Research in Education, 2011), for how over 40 percent of Asian American undergraduates attend community college.
25. Ellen J. Langer, *Mindfulness: 25th Anniversary Edition* (Philadelphia: Da Capo Press, 2014).
26. Marcia B. Baxter Magolda, *Making Their Own Way: Narratives for Transforming Higher Education to Promote Self-Development* (Sterling, VA: Stylus, 2001); Gurin et al., "Diversity and Higher Education," 360–67.
27. Regarding academic gains, see Nida Denson and Mitchell J. Chang, "Racial Diversity Matters: The Impact of Diversity-Related Student Engagement and Institutional Context," *American Educational Research Journal* 46, no. 2 (2009): 322–53; Patricia Gurin, "Expert Report, 'Gratz et al. v. Bollinger, et al.' No. 97-75321 (E.D. Mich.); 'Grutter, et al. v. Bollinger, et al.' No. 97-75928 (E.D. Mich.)," *Equity & Excellence in Education* 32, no. 2 (1999): 36–62; Jiali Luo and David Jamieson-Drake, "A Retrospective Assessment of the Educational Benefits of Interaction Across Racial Boundaries," *Journal of College Student Development* 50, no. 1 (2009): 67–86. Studies documenting cognitive skills and proclivities include Mitchell J. Chang, Alexander W. Astin, and Dongbin Kim, "Cross-Racial Interaction Among Undergraduates: Some Consequences, Causes, and Patterns," *Research in Higher Education* 45, no. 5 (2004): 529–53; Mitchell J. Chang, Nida Denson, Victor Saenz, and Kim Misa, "The Educational Benefits of Sustaining Cross-Racial Interaction Among Undergraduates, *Journal of Higher Education* 77, no. 3 (2006): 430–55; Nida Denson and Shirley Zhang, "The Impact of Student Experiences with Diversity on Developing Graduate Attributes," *Studies in Higher Education* 35, no. 5 (2010): 529–43; Thomas F. Laird, "College Students' Experiences with Diversity and their Effects on Academic Self-confidence, Social Agency, and Disposition Toward Critical Thinking," *Research in Higher Education* 46, no. 4 (2005): 365–87. Regarding prejudice reduction, see Nisha C. Gottfredson, A. T. Panter, Charles E. Daye, Walter F. Allen, and Linda F. Wightman, "The Effects of Educational Diversity in a National Sample of Law Students: Fitting Multilevel Latent Variable Models in Data with Categorical Indicators," *Multivariate Behavioral Research* 44, no. 3 (2009): 305–31; Thomas F. Pettigrew and Linda R. Tropp, "A Meta-Analytic Test of Intergroup Contact Theory," *Journal of Personality and Social Psychology* 90, no. 5 (2006): 751–83; Linda R. Tropp and Thomas F.

Pettigrew, "Relationships Between Intergroup Contact and Prejudice Among Minority and Majority Status Groups," *Psychological Science* 16, no. 12 (2005): 951–57. On increased comfort with people of other races, see Mark Engberg, "Educating the Workforce for the 21st Century: A Cross-Disciplinary Analysis of the Impact of the Undergraduate Experience on Students' Development of a Pluralistic Orientation," *Research in Higher Education* 48, no. 3 (2007): 283–17; Mark Engberg and Sylvia Hurtado, "Developing Pluralistic Skills and Dispositions in College: Examining Racial/Ethnic Group Differences," *Journal of Higher Education* 82, no. 4 (2011): 418–43; Sylvia Hurtado, "The Next Generation of Diversity and Intergroup Relations Research," *Journal of Social Issues* 61, no. 3 (2005): 595–610. On social agency, see Alexander W. Astin, "Diversity and Multiculturalism on the Campus: How Are Students Affected?" *Change* 25, no. 2 (1993): 44–49; Denson and Chang, "Racial Diversity Matters." On retention, see Mitchell J. Chang, "Does Racial Diversity Matter? The Educational Impact of a Racially Diverse Undergraduate Population," *Journal of College Student Development* 40, no. 4 (1999): 377–95. On sense of belonging, see Angela M. Locks, Sylvia Hurtado, Nicholas A. Bowman, and Leticia Oseguera, "Extending Notions of Campus Climate and Diversity to Students' Transition to College," *Review of Higher Education* 31, no. 3 (2008): 257–85. On cultural engagement and understanding, see Anthony L. Antonio, "Diversity and the Influence of Friendship Groups in College," *Review of Higher Education* 25, no. 1 (2001): 63–89; Chang et al., "Educational Benefits of Sustaining." On leadership, see Anthony L. Antonio, "The Role of Interracial Interaction in the Development of Leadership Skills and Cultural Knowledge and Understanding," *Research in Higher Education* 42, no. 5 (2001): 593–617; Denson and Zhang, "The Impact of Student Experiences"; Uma Jayakumar, "Can Higher Education Meet the Needs of an Increasingly Diverse and Global Society?" *Harvard Educational Review* 78, no. 4 (2008): 615–51; Luo and Jamieson-Drake, "A Retrospective Assessment."

28. William A. Smith, Walter R. Allen, and Lynette L. Danley, "'Assume the Position . . . You Fit the Description': Psychosocial Experiences and Racial Battle Fatigue Among African American Male College Students," *American Behavioral Scientist* 51, no. 4 (2007): 551–78, doi:10.1177/0002764207307742.
29. William A. Smith, Man Hung, and Jeremy D. Franklin, "Racial Battle Fatigue and the MisEducation of Black Men: Racial Microaggressions, Societal Problems, and Environmental Stress," *Journal of Negro Education* 80, no. 1 (2011): 63–82; Daniel Solórzano, Miguel Ceja, and Tara Yosso, "Critical Race Theory, Racial Microaggressions, and Campus Racial Climate: The Experience of African American College Students," *Journal of Negro Education* 69, no. 1/2 (2000): 60–73; Derald Wing Sue, Christina M. Capodilupo, Gina C. Torino, Jennifer M. Bucceri, Aisha M. B. Holder, Kevin L. Nadal, and Marta Esquilin, "Racial Microaggressions in Everyday Life: Implications for Clinical Practice," *American Psychologist* 62, no. 4 (2007): 271–86, doi:10.1037/0003-066X.62.4.271; Derald

Wing Sue, Jennifer Bucceri, Annie I. Lin, Kevin L. Nadal, and Gina C. Torino, "Racial Microaggressions and the Asian American Experience," *Cultural Diversity and the Ethnic Minority Psychology* 13, no. 1 (2007); 72–81, doi:10.1037/1099-9809.13.1.72; Tara Yosso, William Smith, Miguel Ceja, and Daniel Solórzano, "Critical Race Theory, Racial Microaggressions, and Campus Racial Climate for Latina/o Undergraduates," *Harvard Educational Review* 79, no. 4 (2009): 659–91, doi:10.17763/haer.79.4.m6867014157m707l. An example of one racial microaggression is asking an Asian American "What's your real name?" because it (1) questions the authenticity or real-ness of one's stated, written, or preferred name; (2) reifies colonial relationships and subordination of students of color; and (3) presumes that Asian Americans and other students of color are perpetually foreign or never American *enough*. Of course "where are you from?" is the classic Asian American-related microaggression, but I can personally attest that there are few things more disorienting than introducing yourself in plain English and having someone ask you what your real name is.

30. Claude M. Steele, *Whistling Vivaldi: How Stereotypes Affect Us and What We Can Do*, Issues of Our Time Series (New York: W. W. Norton, 2010).
31. I attend a predominantly Asian American church where a number of people tend to vote differently than I do, and being in the greater Washington, DC, area, we are never far from the country's politics and atmosphere of polarization. I am not sure I could be constantly immersed in such an intimate environment with people who shared *both* a different race/ethnicity and political orientation—it would just be too taxing. Having, for a slice of my week, a community where many of us share one thing (race) makes it easier to navigate difference in another area (political orientation). And this community does not make up my entire week. Most of my week is spent in a workplace where I am a racial/ethnic minority. Thanks to the laudable, intentional efforts of the University of Maryland to diversify its student body and faculty, this is not the absolute hardest place to be an East Asian American, but I still get reminded of my subordinate status in subtle and sometimes less subtle ways. And it's often tiring. Having another space—my church community—where I do not have to think about race in a way where my alerts and defenses are constantly up makes a world of difference in my ability to persist in another environment that can be more challenging.
32. Bowman and Park, "Interracial Contact on College Campuses."
33. See, for example, Elizabeth Page-Gould, Rodolfo Mendoza-Denton, and Wendy Berry Mendes, "Stress and Coping in Interracial Contexts: The Influence of Race-Based Rejection Sensitivity and Cross-Group Friendship in Daily Experiences of Health," *Journal of Social Issues* 70, no. 2 (2014): 256–78, doi:10.1111/josi.12059; Elizabeth Page-Gould, Rodolfo Mendoza-Denton, Jan M. Alegre, and John O. Siy, "Understanding the Impact of Cross-Group Friendship on Interactions with Novel Outgroup Members," *Journal of Personality and Social*

Psychology 98, no. 5 (2010): 775–93, doi:10.1037/a0017880; Rodolfo Mendoza-Denton and Elizabeth Page-Gould, "Can Cross-Group Friendships Influence Minority Students' Well-Being at Historically White Universities?" *Psychological Science* 19, no. 9 (2008): 933–39, doi:10.1111/j.1467-9280.2008.02179.x.

34. Cited source is Rodolfo Mendoza-Denton, Geraldine Downey, Valerie Purdie, Angelina Davis, and Janina Pietrzak, "Sensitivity to Status-Based Rejection: Implications for African-American Students' College Experience," *Journal of Personality and Social Psychology* 83, no.4 (2002): 896–918. Mendoza-Denton and Page-Gould, "Can Cross-Group Friendships Influence Minority Students' Well-Being at Historically White Universities?" 937–38.
35. Mark S. Granovetter, "The Strength of Weak Ties," *American Journal of Sociology* 78, no. 6 (1973): 1360–80, doi:10.1086/225469.

CHAPTER 2

1. Nicholas A. Bowman and Julie J. Park, "Interracial Contact on College Campuses: Comparing and Contrasting Predictors of Cross-Racial Interaction and Interracial Friendship," *Journal of Higher Education* 85, no. 5 (2014): 679, doi:10.1080/00221546.2014.11777344; Young K. Kim, Julie J. Park, and Katie Koo, "Testing Self-Segregation," *Research in Higher Education* 56, no. 1 (2015): 68.
2. Elizabeth Stearns, Claudia Buchmann, and Kara Bonneau, "Interracial Friendships in the Transition to College: Do Birds of a Feather Flock Together Once They Leave the Nest?" *Sociology of Education* 82, no. 2 (2009): 191, doi:10.1177/003804070908200204.
3. A listing of studies that found a negative effect on general interracial interaction include Anthony L. Antonio, "Diversity and the Influence of Friendship Groups in College," *Review of Higher Education* 25, no. 1 (2001): 79; Victor B. Saenz, Hoi Ning Ngai, and Sylvia Hurtado, "Factors Influencing Positive Interactions Across Race for African American, Asian American, Latino, and White College Students," *Research in Higher Education* 48, no. 1 (2007): 25–34, doi:10.1007/s11162-006-9026-3; and Victor B. Saenz, "Breaking the Segregation Cycle: Examining Students' Pre-College Racial Environments and College Diversity Experiences," *Review of Higher Education* 34, no. 1 (2010): 17.
4. James Sidanius, Colette Van Laar, Shana Levin, and Stacey Sinclair, "Ethnic Enclaves and the Dynamics of Social Identity on the College Campus: The Good, the Bad, and the Ugly," *Journal of Personality and Social Psychology* 87, no. 1 (2004): 105, doi:10.1037/0022-3514.87.1.96.
5. There's a lot to unpack in this statement!
6. Julie J. Park, "Race and the Greek System in the 21st Century: Centering the Voices of Asian American Women," *NASPA Journal* 45, no. 1 (2008): 111–12, doi:10.2202/1949-6605.1909.
7. Tyler Kingkade, "Oklahoma Frat Boys Caught Singing 'There Will Never Be a N***** in SAE,'" *Huffington Post*, March 8, 2015, http://www.huffingtonpost

.com/2015/03/08/frat-racist-sae-oklahoma_n_6828212.html.

8. Meagan Engle, "Sororities' Drunken Actions Shock Miami Alumni, Students," *Dayton Daily News*, May 17, 2010, http://www.daytondailynews.com/news/local/sororities-drunken-actions-shock-miami-alumni-students/toY6eV0M9wDOAJYUerndYI/.
9. Julie J. Park, "Clubs and the Campus Racial Climate: Student Organizations and Interracial Friendship in College," *Journal of College Student Development* 55, no. 7 (2014): 651, doi:10.1353/csd.2014.0076. Thank you to Princeton University for making the NLSF data publicly available.
10. Park, "Race and the Greek System in the 21st Century," 122–25; Jeanette Snider and Julie J. Park, "Walking a Tightrope: Multiracial Women in Racially Homogenous Sororities at a Predominately White University" (roundtable presentation, Association for the Study of Higher Education annual conference, Houston, November 2017).
11. Daniel J. Simons and Christopher F. Chabris, "Gorillas in Our Midst: Sustained Inattentional Blindness for Dynamic Events" *Perception* 29, no. 9 (1999).
12. Chabris and Simons's excellent book details the limitations of mental shortcuts. See Christopher F. Chabris and Daniel J. Simons, *The Invisible Gorilla and Other Ways Our Intuitions Deceive Us* (New York: Crown, 2010); and the video is available at www.theinvisiblegorilla.com.
13. Alfred McClung Lee, *Fraternities Without Brotherhood: A Study of Prejudice on the American Campus* (Boston: Beacon Press, 1995), 93.
14. Park, "Clubs and the Campus Racial Climate," 651.
15. Ibid., 651. According to NLSF data, 32.8 percent, 74.4 percent, and 75.8 percent of students active in Greek life who are Black, Latinx, or Asian American, respectively, participate in groups that they characterize as predominantly White Park, "Clubs and the Campus Racial Climate," 651.
16. Antonio, "Diversity and Friendship Groups," 79; Saenz, Ngai, and Hurtado, "Positive Interactions Across Race," 25–34; Sidanius et al., "Ethnic Enclaves and the Dynamics of Social Identity," 105.
17. Eduardo Bonilla-Silva, *Racism Without Racists: Colorblind Racism and the Persistence of Racial Inequality in America* (Lanham, MD: Rowman & Littlefield, 2014).
18. Sylvia Hurtado, Jeffrey F. Milem, Alma Clayton-Pederson, and Walter R. Allen, "Enhancing Campus Climates for Racial/Ethnic Diversity," *Review of Higher Education* 21, no. 3 (1998): 279–302.
19. Park and Kim, "Interracial Friendship, Structural Diversity, and Peer Groups," *Review of Higher Education* 37, no. 1 (2013): 1–24.
20. For a fuller explanation of these dynamics, see Julie J. Park, Nida Denson, and Nicholas A. Bowman, "Does Socioeconomic Diversity Make a Difference? Examining the Effects of Racial and Socioeconomic Diversity on the Campus Climate for Diversity," *American Educational Research Journal* 50, no. 3 (2013): 466–96.
21. Park, "Race and the Greek System in the 21st Century," 122–25.

22. Julie J. Park, "It Takes a Village (or an Ethnic Economy): The Varying Roles of Socioeconomic Status, Religion, and Social Capital in SAT Preparation for Chinese and Korean American Students," *American Educational Research Journal* 49, no. 4 (2012): 624–50, doi:10.3102/0002831211425609; Min Zhou and Carl L. Bankston III, *Growing Up American: How Vietnamese Children Adapt to Life in the United States* (New York: Russell Sage Foundation, 1998).
23. Scott Thumma, "Racial Diversity Increasing in U.S. Congregations," *HuffingtonPost.com*, March 24, 2013, http://www.huffingtonpost.com/scott-thumma-phd/racial-diversity-increasing-in-us-congregations_b_2944470.html.
24. Alexander Astin, Helen Astin, and Jennifer A. Lindholm. *The Spiritual Lives of College Students: A National Study of College Students' Search for Meaning and Purpose* (Los Angeles: UCLA Higher Education Research Institute, 2004), http://spirituality.ucla.edu/docs/reports/Spiritual_Life_College_Students_Full_Report.pdf.
25. Park, "Clubs and the Campus Racial Climate," 651.
26. Ibid., 653; Julie J. Park, "When Race and Religion Collide: The Effect of Religion on Interracial Friendship in College," *Journal of Diversity in Higher Education* 5, no. 1 (2012): 8–21; Julie J. Park and Young K. Kim, "Interracial Friendship, Structural Diversity, and Peer Groups: Patterns in Greek, Religious, and Ethnic Student Organizations," *Review of Higher Education* 37, no. 1 (2013): 1–24.
27. Julie J. Park and Nicholas A. Bowman, "Religion as Bridging or Bonding Social Capital: Race, Religion, and Cross-Racial Interaction for College Students," *Sociology of Education* 88, no. 1 (2015): 20–37.
28. Paul A. Bramadat, *The Church on the World's Turf: An Evangelical Christian Group at a Secular University* (New York: Oxford University Press, 2000); Alyssa Rockenbach, "The Effects of Involvement in Campus Religious Communities on College Student Adjustment and Development," *Journal of College and Character* 8, no. 3 (2007): 1–25, doi:10.2202/1940-1639.1178; Peter Magolda and Kelsey Ebben Gross, *It's All About Jesus! Faith as an Oppositional Collegiate Subculture* (Sterling, VA: Stylus, 2009).
29. Julie J. Park, Jonathan W. Lew, and Warren Chiang, "Hybrid Faith, Hybrid Identities: Asian American Evangelical Christian Students on College Campuses," in *The Misrepresented Minority: New Insights on Asian Americans and Pacific Islanders, and the Implications for Higher Education*, ed. Samuel D. Museus, Dina C. Maramba, and Robert T. Teranishi (Sterling, VA: Stylus, 2013), 165–81.
30. Alyssa N. Bryant, "The Impact of Campus Context, College Encounters, and Religious/Spiritual Struggle on Ecumenical Worldview Development," *Research in Higher Education* 52, no. 5 (2011): 446–54, doi:10.1007/s11162-010-9206-z.
31. Julie J. Park, *When Diversity Drops: Race, Religion, and Affirmative Action in Higher Education* (New Brunswick, NJ: Rutgers University Press, 2013), 69–80.
32. Korie Edwards, *Elusive Dream: The Power of Race in Interracial Churches* (New York: Oxford University Press, 2008).
33. As captured by Michael Emerson and Christian Smith, *Divided by Faith: Evangelical Religion and the Problem of Race in America* (New York: Oxford University Press, 2000).

34. Sidanius et al., "Ethnic Enclaves and the Dynamics of Social Identity," 96. Interestingly, the students surveyed were the entering class of 1996, one of the last to be admitted prior to Proposition 209, California's affirmative action ban, meaning that the student body was an undeniably more diverse UCLA than exists today.

CHAPTER 3

1. Richard D. Kahlenberg, *The Remedy: Class, Race, and Affirmative Action* (New York: Basic Books, 1996).
2. Sheryll D. Cashin, *Place Not Race: A New Vision of Opportunity in America* (Boston: Beacon Press, 2014). For a critique of Cashin's arguments, see Richard Rothstein, "The Colorblind Blind," *American Prospect*, June 22, 2014, http://prospect.org/article/race-or-class-future-affirmative-action-college-campus.
3. Conor Friedersdorf, "Barack Obama: Affirmative Action's Best Poster Child?" *The Atlantic*, April 28, 2011, https://www.theatlantic.com/politics/archive/2011/04/barack-obama-affirmative-actions-best-poster-child/237990/.
4. Laura Sullivan, Tatjana Meschede, Lars Dietrich, and Thomas Shapiro, *The Racial Wealth Gap: Why Policy Matters* (New York: Demos, 2015), 1–5, http://www.demos.org/sites/default/files/publications/RacialWealthGap_1.pdf.
5. *Left Behind: Unequal Opportunity in Higher Education: A Century Foundation Guide to the Issues*, Reality Check Series (New York: The Century Foundation, 2004), 9, https://tcf.org/assets/downloads/tcf-leftbehindrc.pdf.
6. Thomas J. Espenshade and Alexandria Walton Radford, *No Longer Separate, Not Yet Equal: Race and Class in Elite College Admission and Campus Life* (Princeton, NJ: Princeton University Press, 2009), 100. At first glance, Espenshade and Radford's analysis for the overall sample does not indicate much of an advantage attributed to social class for the average student in the sample, although there are significant interaction terms (variables that consider the intersection between race and class) for low-income students of color buried near the end of the analysis. When you scan the additional analysis, which separated out race/ethnicity and institutional type (private versus public), the bump for low-income students of color reveals itself. Anyone who runs data on people of color understands that sometimes the big story can get lost when everyone gets lumped together, and the nuances are easily missed. In this case, not only does disaggregating by race/ethnicity help, but so does dividing the sample by institutional type, showing that the bump for low-income students of color is sizeable at private institutions.
7. Jennifer Giancola and Richard D. Kahlenberg, *True Merit: Ensuring Our Brightest Students Have Access to Our Best Colleges and Universities* (Lansdowne, VA: Jack Kent Cooke Foundation, 2016), http://www.jkcf.org/assets/1/7/JKCF_true_merit_report.pdf.
8. Ibid., 25.
9. William G. Bowen and Derek Bok, *The Shape of the River: Long-Term Consequences*

of Considering Race in College and University Admissions (Princeton, NJ: Princeton University Press, 1998), 341.

10. David A. Schkade and Daniel Kahneman, "Does Living in California Make People Happy? A Focusing Illusion in Judgments of Life Satisfaction," *Psychological Science* 9, no. 5 (1998): 340–46, doi:10.1111/1467-9280.00066.
11. Antonio Moore, "Black Wealth in America Hardly Exists," *Inequality.org*, October 18, 2016, https://inequality.org/research/black-wealth-exists/.
12. Moore, "Black Wealth in America Hardly Exists."
13. Justin T. Pickett, Ted Chiricos, Kristin M. Golden, and Marc Gertz, "Reconsidering the Relationship Between Perceived Neighborhood Racial Composition and Whites' Perceptions of Victimization Risk: Do Racial Stereotypes Matter?" *Criminology* 50, no. 1 (2012): 145–86, doi:10.1111/j.1745-9125.2011.00255.x.
14. Sean F. Reardon, Rachel Baker, Matt Kasman, Daniel Klasik, and Joseph B. Townsend, *Can Socioeconomic Status Substitute for Race in Affirmative Action College Admissions Policies? Evidence from a Simulation Model* (Princeton, NJ: Educational Testing Service, 2015), https://www.ets.org/Media/Research/pdf/reardon_white_paper.pdf.
15. Ibid., 13.
16. Espenshade and Radford, *No Longer Separate*; Matthew N. Gaertner and Melissa Hart, "Considering Class: College Access and Diversity," *Harvard Law and Policy Review* 7 (2013): 367–403.
17. Reardon et al., *Can Socioeconomic Status Substitute for Race*, 13.
18. Ibid., 11.
19. Ibid., 13.
20. Ibid., 12.
21. Ibid., 19, citing Richard Kahlenberg, "Class-Based Affirmative Action," *California Law Review* 84, no. 4, (1996): 1064.
22. Sigal Alon, *Race, Class, and Affirmative Action* (New York: Russell Sage Press, 2015); Elena M. Bernal, Alberto F. Cabrera, and Patrick T. Terenzini, "The Relationship Between Race and SES Status: Implications for Institutional Research and Admissions Policies," *Removing Vestiges* 3 (2000): 6–13; Deborah C. Malamud, "Assessing Class-Based Affirmative Action," *Journal of Legal Education* 47, no. 4 (1997): 452–71.
23. Caroline Hoxby and Christopher Avery, "The Missing 'One-Offs': The Hidden Supply of High-Achieving, Low-Income Students," *Brookings Papers on Economic Activity* 2013, no. 1 (2013): 1–65, https://www.brookings.edu/wp-content/uploads/2016/07/2013a_hoxby.pdf.
24. See commentary from Richard Kahlenberg and representatives from the Jack Kent Cooke Foundation in Paul Fain, "Poverty and Merit," *Inside Higher Ed*, January 12, 2016, https://www.insidehighered.com/news/2016/01/12/high-achieving-low-income-students-remain-rare-most-selective-colleges.
25. Michael N. Bastedo and Allyson Flaster, "Conceptual and Methodological

Problems in Research on College Undermarch," *Educational Research* 43, no. 2 (2014): 96, doi:10.3102/0013189X14523039.

26. In addition to the unpredictability of institutions in admissions, it's also important to consider the unpredictability of students. Undermatching exists in part due to systemic inequality, but it also exists because there are extraordinary complex factors that influence individuals' sense of what is possible, logical, and rational. As Daniel Ariely has written, individuals are predictably irrational, which is one of the underlying premises of the behavioral economics movement. See Daniel Ariely, *Predictably Irrational: The Hidden Forces That Shape Our Decisions* (New York: HarperCollins, 2008). Or, to phrase it another way, people make decisions that may seem irrational to outsiders or conventional wisdom but make perfect sense to them (e.g., the decision for a rural high school valedictorian to stay close to home instead of attend an Ivy League university). Is this always a good thing when it comes to predicting yield in college admissions? No. But it is a real thing.
27. Bastedo and Flaster, "Conceptual and Methodological Problems," 97.
28. Gordon W. Allport, *The Nature of Prejudice* (Cambridge, UK: Addison-Wesley, 1954).
29. For a more thorough explanation of these processes, including how socioeconomic diversity within racial/ethnic groups can foster a more fluid environment for engagement across race, see Julie J. Park, Nida Denson, and Nicholas A. Bowman, "Does Socioeconomic Diversity Make a Difference? Examining the Effects of Racial and Socioeconomic Diversity on the Campus Climate for Diversity," *American Educational Research Journal* 50, no. 3 (2013): 474–77.
30. Ibid., 489.
31. Sullivan et al., *The Racial Wealth Gap*, 1–5.
32. For an excellent overview of the vulnerability of the Black middle class and the effect on educational opportunity, see Rothstein, "The Colorblind Blind." Rothstein aptly comments on the numerous conditions that make middle-class life a fragile status for many African American families.
33. Allport, *The Nature of Prejudice*. For an additional explanation of why this intra-racial diversity is important, see the brief for 823 *Social Scientists as Amicus Curiae in support of the respondent in Fisher v. University of Texas*, 579 U.S. ___ (2016).

CHAPTER 4

1. Charlie Savage, "Justice Dept. to Take on Affirmative Action in College Admissions," *New York Times*, August 1, 2017, https://www.nytimes.com/2017/08/01/us/politics/trump-affirmative-action-universities.html.
2. Isobel Thompson, "With the White House Under Siege, Trump Starts a Culture War," *Vanity Fair*, August 2, 2017, https://www.vanityfair.com/news/2017/08/donald-trump-culture-war-affirmative-action.
3. Screenshot of the website at "#IAmNotYourWedge: Lawsuits Against Harvard

and UNC Assert Anti-Asian Discrimination in Admissions," *ReAppropriate*, http://reappropriate.co/tag/students-for-fair-admissions/.

4. "UC Berkeley Fall Enrollment Data (Fall 2016)," Office of Planning and Analysis, University of California, Berkeley, http://opa.berkeley.edu/uc-berkeley-fall-enrollment-data.
5. Teresa Watanabe, "How UCLA Is Boosting Campus Diversity, Despite the Ban on Affirmative Action," *Los Angeles Times*, June 23, 2016, http://www.latimes.com/local/california/la-me-ucla-diversity-20160620-snap-story.html; "Quick Facts about UCLA," UCLA Undergraduate Admission, http://www.admission.ucla.edu/campusprofile.htm; Watanabe, "How UCLA Is Boosting Campus Diversity."
6. "UCLA Has More NCAA Championships Than Black Male Freshmen," Black Voices, *Huffington Post*, November 8, 2013, http://www.huffingtonpost.com/2013/11/08/ucla-black-enrollment-freshmen_n_4242213.html.
7. "UC San Diego—Fall 2016: Undergraduate Enrollment," Student Research and Information, Institutional Research, Academic Affairs, University of California, San Diego, http://studentresearch.ucsd.edu/_files/stats-data/enroll/ugethnic.pdf.
8. Ibid.
9. Frances Contreras, Thandeka Chapman, Eddie Comeaux, Gloria M. Rodriguez, Malo Hutson, and Eligio Martinez, "Investing in California's African American Students: College Choice, Diversity and Exclusion" (report, University of California Office of the President, San Diego, February 2016), http://iurd.berkeley.edu/research/EXCEL_Report_2016.pdf; J. Douglas Allen-Taylor, "Why Black Students Are Avoiding UC Berkeley," *East Bay Express*, November 6, 2013, https://www.eastbayexpress.com/oakland/why-black-students-are-avoiding-uc-berkeley/Content?oid=3756649.
10. "Top 5 Anti–Affirmative Action Myths About SCA5," *ReAppropriate*, March 7, 2014, http://reappropriate.co/tag/students-for-fair-admissions/.
11. Min Zhou and Susan S. Kim, "Community Forces, Social Capital, and Educational Achievement: The Case of Supplementary Education in the Chinese and Korean Immigrant Communities," *Harvard Educational Review* 76, no. 1 (2006): 1–29, doi:10.17763/haer.76.1.u08t548554882477; Julie J. Park, "It Takes a Village (or an Ethnic Economy): The Varying Roles of Socioeconomic Status, Religion, and Social Capital in SAT Preparation for Chinese and Korean American Students," *American Educational Research Journal* 49, no. 4 (2012): 624–50, doi: 10.3102/0002831211425609.
12. On a related note, I'm guessing that some people were simply unaware of how admissions currently works in the UC system. For many years, until it changed to its present system of holistic admissions, the UC admissions system utilized a point-value system similar to those used in other large and competitive state public higher education systems. Applicants got a certain number of points for GPA, SAT score, being from a certain underrepresented (rural)

region, having exceptional talents or accomplishments, and, before the 1996 passage of Proposition 209, race/ethnicity. Similar point-based systems used in other systems were struck down with the 2003 Supreme Court ruling in *Gratz v. Bollinger*. For more information on comprehensive review in the UC system, see http://admission.universityofcalifornia.edu/counselors/files/comprehensive_review_facts.pdf.

13. Thomas J. Espenshade and Alexandria Walton Radford, *No Longer Separate, Not Yet Equal: Race and Class in Elite College Admission and Campus Life* (Princeton, NJ: Princeton University Press, 2009), 93.
14. Ibid., 67.
15. Harvard is not representative of all institutions, but Espenshade and Radford's findings have been used to argue that discrimination exists in Harvard admissions. The National Study of College Experience (NCSE) institutions have little in common with Harvard on at least two key metrics: the average enrollment of a NCSE sample institution in 2004 was 18,000, with an acceptance rate of 35 percent. Ibid., 10.
16. Scott Jaschik, "The Power of Race," *Inside Higher Ed*, November 3, 2009, https://www.insidehighered.com/news/2009/11/03/elite.
17. Scott Jaschik, "Is It Bias? Is It Legal?" *Inside Higher Ed*, February 3, 2012, https://www.insidehighered.com/news/2012/02/03/federal-probe-raises-new-questions-discrimination-against-asian-american-applicants.
18. Do Asian Americans experience discrimination and bias in society writ large? Absolutely. But this fact doesn't necessarily mean that Asian Americans are being treated unfairly in the selective admissions process. Now might there be some higher expectations for Asian Americans when it comes to standardized tests as a group writ large given that they tend to get higher SAT scores on average—an idea that is not unfounded given that (1) they really do have the highest average scores and (2) many of them participate in a SAT industrial complex that actually uniquely benefits them. Is this fair? If your conception of fairness is limited to the idea that everyone should be assessed exactly the same, maybe not. But if your conception of fairness includes some element of being able to assess accomplishments in the context of opportunity afforded to individuals, maybe it's not such a bad idea. What is fairness, after all? Those who believe that everyone's SAT score should be assessed identically may think it doesn't matter that certain folks (the wealthy and, as an aggregate whole, East Asian Americans) are able to access and benefit from supplemental resources like SAT prep classes at higher rates. But there are others who think that it's not fair in the first place that everyone is being asked to take the same test but that certain groups are able to leverage advantages other groups don't have.
19. Oiyan Poon, in discussion with the author, August 2017.
20. Park, "It Takes a Village," 639.
21. And part of it exists because of the complex infrastructure of the ethnic

economy, which feeds the demand with an ample supply of SAT tutoring businesses specifically catering to Asian Americans. On top of that, research suggests that Asian Americans as an aggregate group are the only racial/ethnic group that experiences significant gains on test prep. As will be explained in the next chapter, despite aggressive advertising which claims that students gain hundreds of points from taking Kaplan or Kumon test prep, studies that use a more appropriate research design to track the effects of test prep indicate that gains are quite minimal overall, except for one group, Asian Americans. Soo-yong Byun and Hyunjoon Park, "The Academic Success of East Asian American Youth: The Role of Shadow Education," *Sociology of Education* 85, no. 1 (2012): 54–55, doi:10.1177/0038040711417009; Julie J. Park and Ann H. Becks, "Who Benefits from SAT Prep? An Examination of High School Context and Race/Ethnicity," *Review of Higher Education* 39, no. 1 (2015): 14, doi:10.1353/rhe.2015.0038.

22. Asian immigrant communities are dense with social capital networks: networks of relationships that support the exchange of information and resources. These networks exert significant pressure on young Asian Americans to perceive certain behaviors as normal—like the idea that it's normal to go to afterschool or summer tutoring. It creates an ethos where parents observe what other parents are doing and attempt to do the same for their children. Ethnic economies, communities, and social capital networks also incubate less tangible but no less important forces like the act of everyone's auntie gossiping about who got what SAT score, who won what violin competition, and who's going where for college.
23. Lee and Zhou, *Asian American Achievement Paradox*, 51–68.
24. I'm looking at Nicholas Kristof, who seems to always be throwing out a variant of this theory every few years in his *New York Times* column, such as in "The Asian Advantage" on October 10, 2015, https://www.nytimes.com/2015/10/11/opinion/sunday/the-asian-advantage.html. For rebuttals, see Janelle S. Wong, "Editorial: The Source of the 'Asian Advantage' Isn't Asian Values," *NBC News*, October 13, 2015, http://www.nbcnews.com/news/asian-america/editorial-source-asian-advantage-isnt-asian-values-n443526; Emil Guillermo, "Nick Kristof's Distasteful Reframing of the Model Minority as 'the Asian Advantage' in the *New York Times*," *Asian American Legal Defense and Education Fund*, October 12, 2015, http://aaldef.org/blog/emil-guillermo-nick-kristofs-distasteful-reframing-of-the-model-minority-as-the-asian-advantage.html; and "When Nicholas Kristof Just Doesn't Get It About Asian Americans," *Reappropriate*, October 13, 2015, http://reappropriate.co/2015/10/when-nicholas-kristof-just-doesnt-get-it-about-asian-americans/.
25. There are major differences within the Asian American community due to social class and ethnicity, but these are some of the dynamics that have come to influence the educational norms facing many South and East Asian

American young people, even though most Asian Americans don't achieve the heavy expectations of the "success frame." Lee and Zhou, *Asian American Achievement Paradox*, 51–68. Remember that about 40 percent of Asian Americans in college attend not Harvard or Berkeley but a community college. Robert Teranishi, *The Relevance of Asian Americans and Pacific Islanders in the College Completion Agenda* (New York: National Commission on Asian American and Pacific Islander Research in Education, 2011), 9, http://care.gseis.ucla.edu/wp-content/uploads/2015/08/2011_CARE_Report.pdf. Lee and Zhou ask the brilliantly simple question: If Asians supposedly value education so much, what percentage of people in China actually graduate with a college degree? The answer is (drumroll) 4 percent (30). This surprised me—and I actually study this for a living! We in America often hear how Asia (and Finland) is kicking our butts when it comes to all of those international math tests. While that might be true, there are also a whole lot of people in China and other countries who aren't going to college.

26. Why a sector of the East and South Asian American populations is so hyped up on test scores and academic competition is a much more complex social process than simply "valuing education." As an aggregate group, Asian Americans have relatively high levels of achievement. It's important to emphasize the word *aggregate*, because when you disaggregate the Asian American population by ethnicity or social class, achievement patterns are all over the map. But when you're just looking at the entire population lumped together, they're doing pretty well. This is not an accident. The immigration policies influencing what Asians have been able to come to the United States are not a random sampling of various Asian countries. Prior to 1965, Asian immigration was a smattering here and a community there, a hodge-podge of laborers, freedom fighters, and aspiring scholars. The Chinese Exclusion Act of 1882 was (until Trump) the only law in US history that specifically banned immigration based on ethnicity. There were other ugly laws that the government used to tamp down the Asian American communities, such as the Alien Land Act, which banned anyone born overseas from owning property. Then, in 1965, everything changed. The US Congress passed an overhaul of immigration laws, which opened the door for much larger waves of immigration, with a particular preference for highly skilled folks from East Asia. This was the wave that brought my father over from Korea in the late 1960s for graduate school at the University of Illinois. This was no random lotto; you had to take and pass a test. Immigration laws became more expansive to allow highly skilled Asian immigrants to come fill positions that US companies were having trouble filling, like doctors to work in rural towns (how our close family friends ended up in New Lebanon, Ohio). Later waves of immigrants from East Asia tended to be more socioeconomically diverse, the extended families of the high achievers, refugees, and people who really did win the lotto to come over: immigration

via family reunification. Because they made up a significant proportion of the Asian American population at the time, the highly educated, post-1965 crowd tended to set the pace and set expectations for future waves of immigrants and their children. They were the cream of the crop in their country, and while many of them came over as humble graduate students, they also came loaded with massive amounts of cultural capital—the habits, dispositions, and expectations of upper-class folks. High educational expectations generally don't just drop out of the sky; they develop over the years when enabled by (relative) generational privilege. Over time, what was originally more of advantage associated with social class became a set of expectations that became a dominant norm within a broader racial/ethnic group, as argued by Lee and Zhou in the *Asian American Achievement Paradox*. Further, East Asian Americans in particular have built an infrastructure to spread and support these high expectations through creating extensive ethnic economies that support tangible resources like SAT tutoring and ethnic newspapers that advertise such services and highlight high-achieving students as role models.

27. Teranishi, *The Relevance of Asian Americans and Pacific Islanders.*
28. The model minority myth is not just a neutral stereotype where people just happen to typecast Asian Americans as nerdy; it functions as a form of anti-Blackness, specifically casting Asian Americans as the "ideal" minority as a way to reinforce oppression against other communities of color. See Oiyan A. Poon, Dian Squire, Corinne Kodama, C., Ajani Byrd, Jason Chan, Lester Manzano, Sara Furr, and Devita Bishundat, "A Critical Review of the Model Minority Myth in Selected Literature on Asian Americans and Pacific Islanders in Higher Education," *Review of Educational Research* 86 no. 2 (2016): 469–502.
29. Espenshade and Radford, *Race and Class*, 95.
30. ChangHwan Kim and Arthur Sakamoto, "The Earnings of Less Educated Asian American Men: Educational Selectivity and the Model Minority Image," *Social Problems* 61, no. 2 (2014): 283–304, doi:10.1525/sp.2014.12029.
31. "Where Do Asian Americans Stand on Affirmative Action?" *National Asian American Survey*, June 24, 2013, http://naasurvey.com/where-do-asian-americans-stand-on-affirmative-action/.
32. Timur Kuran and Cass R. Sunstein, "Availability Cascades and Risk Regulation," *Stanford Law Review* 51, no. 4 (1999): 683.
33. Ibid.
34. Ibid., 688.
35. Ron Unz, "The Myth of American Meritocracy," *The American Conservative*, November 28, 2012, http://www.theamericanconservative.com/articles/the-myth-of-american-meritocracy/.
36. Peter Schmidt, "Asian-American Groups Seek Federal Investigation of Alleged Bias at Harvard," *Chronicle of Higher Education*, May 15, 2015, http://www.chronicle.com/blogs/ticker/asian-american-groups-seek-federal-investigation-

of-alleged-bias-at-harvard/; "Supporters," Asian American Civil Rights, http://asianamericancivilrights.org/supporters.

37. "Where Do Asian Americans Stand on Affirmative Action?"
38. Jeff Yang, "Harvard Lawsuit Is Not What It Seems," CNN, November 24, 2014, http://www.cnn.com/2014/11/24/opinion/yang-harvard-lawsuit/.
39. Her senior year, he won the state championship for Foreign Extemporaneous Speaking, a speech and debate event where participants have to write and memorize a 5 to 7 minute speech on an event in international affairs in 30 minutes.
40. "Top 10 SAT Scores of Athletes in Pro-Sports," *topbet*, July 23, 2013, http://topbet.eu/news/10-athletes-with-highest-sat-scores.html; Ginger Bean, March 27, 2013 (1:12 pm), comment on Prince187, "What Did LeBron Score on the SAT/ACT," *RealGM Basketball Forum*, March 25, 2013, https://forums.realgm.com/boards/viewtopic.php?t=1241051&start=105; Avinash Kunnath, "Jeremy Lin and How Stanford, UCLA, Cal, and the PAC-12 Missed Him," *Pacific Takes*, February 12, 2012, https://www.pacifictakes.com/2012/2/12/2791271/jeremy-lin-stanford-ucla-bruins-cal-harvard-palo-alto-recruiting.
41. As quoted in the complaint for *Students for Fair Admissions v. President and Fellows of Harvard College* (14-cv-14176-adb), 807 F.2d 1st Cir. D. Mass., filed November 17, 2014, https://studentsforfairadmissions.org/wp-content/uploads/2014/11/SFFA-v.-Harvard-Complaint.pdf.
42. "SAT Subject Tests Percentile Ranks: 2015 College-Bound Seniors," The College Board, 2015, https://secure-media.collegeboard.org/digitalServices/pdf/sat/sat-percentile-ranks-subject-tests-2015.pdf.
43. "Admissions Statistics: Harvard Admitted Students Profile," Harvard College Admissions and Financial Aid, https://college.harvard.edu/admissions/admissions-statistics.
44. Ibid.
45. "Our Selection Process: Applicant Profile (as of August 2017)," Undergraduate Admission, Stanford University, http://admission.stanford.edu/apply/selection/profile.html.
46. "Admission Statistics: Statistics for Applicants to the Class of 2021 (as of July 15, 2017)," Undergraduate Admission, Princeton University, July 15, 2017, https://admission.princeton.edu/how-apply/admission-statistics.
47. "By the Numbers 2017: Admissions and Financial Aid," *Harvard Crimson*, http://features.thecrimson.com/2013/frosh-survey/admissions.html.
48. That's within our budget, of course.
49. For their acknowledgment that their research does not answer the question of whether discrimination exists against Asian Americans, see Espenshade and Radford, *Race and Class*, 95.
50. Jerry Kang, "Negative Action Against Asian Americans: The Internal Instability of Dworkin's Defense of Affirmative Action," *Harvard Civil Rights–Civil Liberties Law Review* 31 (1996): 1–47.

51. Jaschik, "The Power of Race"; Espenshade and Radford, *Race and Class*, 95.
52. *Students for Fair Admissions v. President and Fellows of Harvard College*, 53–55.
53. Ibid., 55.
54. Damon Hewitt, "The Truth About New York City's Elite High Schools," *New York Times*, March 22, 2017, https://www.nytimes.com/2017/03/22/opinion/the-truth-about-new-york-citys-elite-high-schools.html?_r=0; Elizabeth A. Harris and Ford Fessenden, "The Broken Promises of Choice in New York City Schools," *New York Times*, May 5, 2017, https://www.nytimes.com/2017/05/05/nyregion/school-choice-new-york-city-high-school-admissions.html?_r=0.
55. *Students for Fair Admissions v. President and Fellows of Harvard College*, 45.
56. Ibid., 46.
57. An intriguing study by researchers at the University of Michigan provides further context for this dynamic. They found that East Asian Americans were more likely than Whites to want to attend a more prestigious university even if they would be considered a below-average student there than to attend a less prestigious institution where they would be a stronger student relative to their peers. This dynamic helps us understand why applications from Asian Americans to places to Harvard might be especially high and why there the application sending rate from Asian Americans is higher than the actual percentage of Asian Americans admitted to Harvard, because even students who recognize that they are below average still want to attend what they view as an exceptionally prestigious university. See Kaidi Wu, Stephen M. Garcia, and Shirli Kopelman, "Frogs, Ponds, and Culture: Variations in Entry Decisions," *Social Psychological and Personality Science* (forthcoming), doi:10.1177/1948550617706731.
58. *Students for Fair Admissions v. President and Fellows of Harvard College*, 46.
59. Espenshade and Radford, *No Longer Separate, Not Yet Equal*, 85–86.
60. Espenshade and Radford, *Race and Class*, 99–100.
61. Figure 3.9 in ibid., 98.
62. Emily Pronin, Daniel Y. Lin, and Lee Ross, "The Bias Blind Spot: Perceptions of Bias in Self Versus Others," *Personality and Social Psychology Bulletin* 28, no. 3 (2002): 369–81, doi:10.1177/0146167202286008.
63. See Espenshade and Radford, *Race and Class*, 99–101. I wanted to blame my missing this on it being buried in footnotes, but, nope, it's there in plain sight.
64. My missing the finding on low-income Asian Americans is yet another "gorilla at the basketball game" moment. See chapter 2 this volume.
65. *Students for Fair Admissions v. President and Fellows of Harvard College*, 45.
66. The math of how I got there begins with an estimate of the proportion of legacies who are White, along with the fact that 79.3 percent of recruited athletes that year were White; recruited athletes made up 12.5 percent of the overall first-year student body. Add the two numbers together and it ends up being about one-third of the White undergraduate enrollment, by conservative estimates. To provide more detail, Harvard Dean of Admissions and

Financial Aid William Fitzsimmons reported in 2011 that about 12–13 percent of each Harvard class is made up of legacy students, as reported in Justin C. Worland, "Legacy Admit Rate at 30 Percent," *Harvard Crimson*, May 11, 2011, http://www.thecrimson.com/article/2011/5/11/admissions-fitzsimmons-legacy-legacies/. In the 2018 *Harvard Crimson* survey of first-year students, 15.9 percent reported having at least one parent who attended Harvard as an undergraduate. "Class of 2018 by the Numbers," *Harvard Crimson*, http://features.thecrimson.com/2014/freshman-survey/makeup/. Still, to be conservative, I use Fitzsimmons's estimate of 12 percent. In the 2014 Crimson Graduating Senior Survey, about 80 percent of legacy respondents were White. Rebecca D. Robbins, "The Class of 2014 by the Numbers," *Harvard Crimson*, n.d., http://features.thecrimson.com/2014/senior-survey/. I use an even more conservative estimate of 66 percent of legacies being White for the sake of this calculation. Thus, if 66 percent of legacies are White, that would be about 8 percent of the Harvard class who are White legacies. Data on the Class of 2017 indicates that 12.5 percent of the class were recruited athletes, and 79.3 percent of such athletes were White; 79.3 percent of 12.5 percent is 9.9 percent, and thus, about 9.9 percent of the Harvard class would be made up of White recruited athletes. Add 9.9 and 8 and you get about 18 percent of Harvard's student body being made up of White legacies and recruited athletes. "The Class of 2017 by the Numbers," *Harvard Crimson*, n.d., http://features.thecrimson.com/2013/frosh-survey/makeup.html. Of course, to reiterate, being a legacy or athlete may not be the primary reason all of these students were admitted, although such students often receive special consideration. Harvard's graduating Class of 2015 was 43 percent White, which would mean that about 41 percent of Harvard White students were legacies or athletes (18 divided by 43). Harvard University Office of Institutional Research, "Degrees Awarded: Demographics," n.d., https://oir.harvard.edu/fact-book/degrees-awarded-demographics. I'll lowball it even a little more to take into consideration that there may be students who are both legacies and recruited athletes, as well as other factors such as nonrespondents in the *Crimson* student surveys (however, it is the same data referenced in the SFFA lawsuit) and come up with the estimate that about one-third of Harvard White students receive some special consideration in the admissions process due to being a legacy or recruited athlete. I also discuss this issue in Julie J. Park, "The White Admissions Advantage: Unfair, but Different from Discrimination against Asian Americans," *Huffington Post*, March 25, 2015, http://www.huffingtonpost.com/julie-j-park/the-white-admissions-adva_b_6932670.html.

67. Julie J. Park, "The Misleading Lawsuit Accusing Harvard of Bias Against Asian Americans," *Washington Post*, January 2, 2015, https://www.washingtonpost.com/opinions/the-misleading-lawsuit-accusing-harvard-of-bias-against-asian-americans/2015/01/02/cc7a7c52-91e5-11e4-ba53-a477d66580ed_story.html?utm_term=.935590b51d02.

68. They've since expanded it a bit to encompass students with a "deep-seated commitment to diversity and social justice." "Merit Scholarship Opportunities: Chancellor's Scholars," Vanderbilt University, http://www.vanderbilt.edu/scholarships/chancellor.php.
69. "The Vanderbilt Profile," Vanderbilt University, https://admissions.vanderbilt.edu/profile/#undergradstudentpopulation.
70. The Cayugha's Waiters, an acapella group at Cornell, even performs the song "We Didn't Go to Harvard" to the tune of Billy Joel's "We Didn't Start the Fire." "Applicant" could be attending Cornell and singing that song right now!

CHAPTER 5

1. Regina Deil-Amen and Tenisha Tevis, "Circumscribed Agency: The Relevance of Standardized College Entrance Exams for Low SES High School Students," *Review of Higher Education* 33, no. 2 (2010): 141–75.
2. Samuel D. Museus, Shaun R. Harper, and Andrew H. Nichols, "Racial Differences in the Formation of Postsecondary Educational Expectations: A Structural Model," *Teachers College Record* 112, no. 3 (2010): 811–42.
3. Prudence L. Carter, *Keepin' It Real: School Success Beyond Black and White* (New York: Oxford University Press, 2005).
4. Julie J. Park, "It Takes a Village (or an Ethnic Economy): The Varying Roles of Socioeconomic Status, Religion, and Social Capital in SAT Preparation for Chinese and Korean American Students," *American Educational Research Journal* 49, no. 4 (2012): 639, doi:10.3102/0002831211425609.
5. Ibid., 639.
6. Elizabeth A. Harris and Ford Fessenden, "The Broken Promises of Choice in New York City Schools," *New York Times*, May 5, 2017, https://www.nytimes.com/2017/05/05/nyregion/school-choice-new-york-city-high-school-admissions.html?_r=0. At the time of writing, there were recent proposals to change the admissions process for the most elite selective public high schools. Thus, the future of test-only based admissions is unknown.
7. Park, "It Takes a Village," 639. For a detailed account of how ethnic economies support the infrastructure of test prep, see Min Zhou and Susan S. Kim, "Community Forces, Social Capital, and Educational Achievement: The Case of Supplementary Education in the Chinese and Korean Immigrant Communities," *Harvard Educational Review* 76, no. 1 (2006): 1–29. For further detail on how ethnic economies facilitate interclass contact among immigrants and their children, see Min Zhou, *Contemporary Chinese America: Immigration, Ethnicity, and Community Transformation* (Philadelphia: Temple University Press, 2009). For more on the link between interclass contact among immigrants and the pervasiveness of SAT prep, see Park, "It Takes a Village."
8. For excellent examples documenting the effects of social class among Asian Americans, see Vivian S. Louie, *Compelled to Excel: Immigration, Education, and*

Opportunity Among Chinese Americans (Palo Alto, CA: Stanford University Press, 2004); and Jamie Lew, *Asian Americans in Class: Charting the Achievement Gap Among Korean American Youth* (New York: Teachers College Press, 2006). While the effect of social class is pronounced, there are certain forces that buffer its influence. One is *stereotype boost*, where Asian Americans (or other groups) are positively stereotyped and priming these stereotypes can enhance academic performance. For more on stereotype boost, see Margaret J. Shih, Todd L. Pittinsky, and Geoffrey C. Ho, "Stereotype Boost: Positive Outcomes from the Activation of Positive Stereotypes," in *Stereotype Threat: Theory, Process, and Application, eds.* Michael Inzlicht and Toni Schmader (New York: Oxford University Press, 2012), 141–56. Don't get me wrong, I think and know from personal experience that Asian Americans experience plenty of discrimination in everyday life. The effect of "positive" stereotyping can be pernicious, leading to pressures imposed on Asian American youth, resulting in serious mental health challenges and intergenerational conflict. Yet, the effect of stereotyping also results in a phenomenon where Asian Americans are often given the benefit of the doubt, whether they actually deserve it or not, when it comes to academics. In *The Asian American Achievement Paradox* (New York: Russell Sage Foundation, 2015), sociologists Jennifer Lee and Min Zhou capture the voices of Asian Americans recounting times when teachers assumed they could do the work or gave them the benefit of the doubt. In contrast, we know that this "benefit of the doubt" is less likely to be given to other youth of color, particularly low-income, urban youth.

9. Lee and Zhou, *The Asian American Achievement Paradox*, 51–68. Lee and Zhou call socialization into a set of cognitive schemas affecting East Asian Americans "the success frame."
10. Patricia M. McDonough and Shannon Calderone, "The Meaning of Money Perceptual Differences Between College Counselors and Low-Income Families About College Costs and Financial Aid," *American Behavioral Scientist* 49, no. 12 (2006): 1704. The authors provide a helpful overview of the concept of habitus.
11. Donelson R. Forsyth, *Group Dynamics, 5th ed. (New York: Cengage Learning, 2009)*, 317.
12. Other initiatives that offer fixes to key issues in access to opportunity also can fall short. Take the Kalamazoo Promise, a widely heralded initiative where any child attending Kalamazoo Public Schools will have their college paid for. An amazing program, no doubt, and college enrollment rates in the district overall have gone up, no small feat. Yet high school graduation rates for African American males remain at 44 percent, and overall college graduation rates remain a significant challenge. A great program, yes, but just one piece of the puzzle. There is a growing effort for foundations to also begin targeting support for early childhood education. Ted C. Fishman, "Why These Kids Get a Free Ride to College," *New York Times Magazine*, September 13, 2012, http://www.nytimes.com/2012/09/16/magazine/kalamazoo-mich-the-city-that-pays-for-college.html.

13. Thomas J. Espenshade and Alexandria Walton Radford, *No Longer Separate, Not Yet Equal: Race and Class in Elite College Admission and Campus Life* (Princeton, NJ: Princeton University Press, 2009), 98–100.
14. See Alexandria Walton Radford, *Top Student, Top School? How Social Class Shapes Where Valedictorians Go to College* (Chicago: University of Chicago Press, 2013).
15. Ah, participation grades—the low-hanging fruit of academia.
16. Derek C. Briggs, "Preparation for College Admission Exams" (Discussion Paper Series, National Association for College Admission Counseling, Arlington, VA, 2009), https://files.eric.ed.gov/fulltext/ED505529.pdf.
17. To quote from a report commissioned by the National Association for College Admissions Counseling by Derek Briggs in 2009: "Regardless, the question of interest would not be whether students increase their scores from one testing to the next, but whether such an increase can be validly attributed to the coaching that preceded it. In general, to make such an attribution requires the availability of a comparable group of students that take the test twice but are not coached. If the score gains of coached students are significantly larger than the score gains of uncoached students, this would constitute a positive coaching effect. Since uncoached students will on average also improve their scores just by retaking the test, an estimate of the effect of coaching will always be smaller than the observed score gains for coached students. For more on this distinction between gains and effects that is the root of many common misconceptions, see Powers and Camara, 1999; Briggs, 2004." Briggs, "Preparation for College Admission Exams," 11. I and many others personally don't think that randomized controlled trials (RCTs) are the only way of documenting whether something "works" or not, and RCTs are not always feasible or realistic to set up. But when they are, it's best when they are complimented by other research methods, such as qualitative methods that can capture the nuance and gradients behind why something may or may not be working.
18. Larry Gordon, "Free Khan Academy SAT Tutorials Boost Scores, Study Finds," *EdSource*, May 8, 2017, https://edsource.org/2017/free-khan-academy-sat-tutorials-boost-scores-study-finds/581450.
19. Briggs, "Preparation for College Admission Exams," 12.
20. Ben Domingue and Derek C. Briggs, "Using Linear Regression and Propensity Score Matching to Estimate the Effect of Coaching on the SAT," *Multiple Linear Regression Viewpoints* 35, no. 1 (2009): 12–29.
21. Soo-yong Byun and Hyunjoon Park, "The Academic Success of East Asian American Youth: The Role of Shadow Education," *Sociology of Education* 85, no. 1 (2012): 54–55, doi:10.1177/0038040711417009.
22. Julie J. Park and Ann H. Becks, "Who Benefits from SAT Prep? An Examination of High School Context and Race/Ethnicity," *Review of Higher Education* 39, no. 1 (2015): 14, doi:10.1353/rhe.2015.0038.
23. Christopher Avery, "Evaluation of the College Possible Program: Results from

a Randomized Controlled Trial" (Working Paper No. 19562, National Bureau of Economic Research, Cambridge, MA, 2013), doi:10.3386/w19562.

24. Byun and Park, "The Academic Success of East Asian American Youth," 52.
25. Lee and Zhou, *The Asian American Achievement Paradox*, 51–68.
26. Park, "It Takes a Village," 639; Byun and Park, "The Academic Success of East Asian American Youth," 54.
27. Briggs, "Preparation for College Admission Exams."
28. The fact that 40 percent of first-time, full-time Black freshmen reported taking a prep course may point to the high level of coaching among the subsample of Black students enrolled at traditional, four-year institutions, versus the broader population. Thus, rates of participation are higher than one might expect, but, overall, benefits appear to be inconsistent across the population. See Park, "It Takes a Village"; and Sigal Alon, "Racial Differences in Test Preparation Strategies: A Commentary on Shadow Education, American Style: Test Preparation, the SAT and College Enrollment," *Social Forces* 89, no. 2 (2010): 463–74, doi:10.1353/sof.2010.0053.
29. Domingue and Briggs, "Effect of Coaching on the SAT," 23.
30. Charles Rooney and Bob Schaeffer, *Test Scores Do Not Equal Merit: Enhancing Equity and Excellence in College Admissions by Deemphasizing SAT and ACT Results* (Cambridge, MA: National Center for Fair and Open Testing [FairTest]), 1998, 1–7; Lani Guinier, *The Tyranny of the Meritocracy: Democratizing Higher Education in America* (Boston: Beacon Press, 2015).
31. Paul Pringle, "College Board Scores with Critics of SAT Analogies," *Los Angeles Times*, July 27, 2003, http://articles.latimes.com/2003/jul/27/local/me-sat27.
32. "The *Princeton Review* Comments on the SAT Changes Announced by the College Board on March 5" (press release), *Princeton Review*, March 7, 2014, https://www.princetonreview.com/press/sat-changes.
33. The Khan Academy program has been lauded as a success; however, the use of pre- and postscores are unable to indicate an effective treatment or causality. Catherine Gewertz, "College Board Reports Score Gains from Free SAT Practice," *Education Week*, May 8, 2017, http://blogs.edweek.org/edweek/high_school_and_beyond/2017/05/college_board_reports_score_gains_from_free_sat_practice.html.
34. "George W. Bush's Speech to the NAACP," *Washington Post*, July 10, 2000, http://www.washingtonpost.com/wp-srv/onpolitics/elections/bushtext071000.htm.
35. Condoleezza Rice, *Extraordinary, Ordinary People: A Memoir of Family* (New York: Three Rivers Press, 2010), 138.
36. For case studies which highlight institutions that have made the successful transition to SAT optional, see Rooney and Schaeffer, *Test Scores Do Not Equal Merit*, 15–40.
37. Valerie Strauss, "What One College Discovered When It Stopped Accepting SAT Scores," *Washington Post*, September 25, 2015, https://www.washingtonpost

.com/news/answer-sheet/wp/2015/09/25/what-one-college-discovered-when-it-stopped-accepting-satact-scores/?utm_term=.683de50f22aa.

38. Sigal Alon and Marta Tienda, "Diversity, Opportunity, and the Shifting Meritocracy in Higher Education," *American Sociological Review* 72, no. 4 (2007): 487–511; also see Scott Jaschik, "Provocative Theory on Merit," *Inside Higher Ed*, July 18, 2007, https://www.insidehighered.com/news/2007/07/18/sat.
39. Catherine Horn and Stella M. Flores, "Percent Plans in College Admissions: A Comparative Analysis of Three States' Experiences" (report, Harvard Civil Rights Project, Cambridge, MA, February 2003), http://files.eric.ed.gov/fulltext/ED472484.pdf; Catherine Horn and Stella M. Flores, "When Policy Opportunity Is Not Enough: College Access and Enrollment Patterns among Texas Percent Plan Eligible Students," *Journal of Applied Research on Children: Informing Policy for Children at Risk* 3, no. 2 (2012): 9, http://digitalcommons.library.tmc.edu/childrenatrisk/vol3/iss2/9.
40. Saul Geiser, "The Growing Correlation between Race and SAT Scores: New Findings from California" (Research and Occasional Paper Series No. 10.15, Center for Studies in Higher Education, University of California, Berkeley, October 2015), https://cshe.berkeley.edu/sites/default/files/publications/rops.cshe.10.15.geiser.racesat.10.26.2015.pdf.
41. Lorelle Espinosa, Matthew Gaertner, and Gary Orfield, *Race, Class, and College Access: Achieving Diversity in a Shifting Landscape* (Washington, DC: American Council on Education), 2005, 23, http://www.acenet.edu/news-room/Documents/Race-Class-and-College-Access-Achieving-Diversity-in-a-Shifting-Legal-Landscape.pdf.
42. Ibid., 21. Right before this book went to press, the University of Chicago announced its plan to go SAT-optional, so we will see if more highly selective and other colleges follow.
43. There is a growing body of research examining the effectiveness of SAT-optional. The test prep industry supported the release of a volume critiquing SAT-optional, see Jack Buckley, Lynn Letukas, and Ben Wildavsky, eds., *Measuring Success: Testing Grades and the Future of Colllege Admission* (Baltimore: Johns Hopkins University Press, 2017). A recent report supporting SAT-optional is Steven T. Syverson, Valerie W. Franks, and William Hiss, *Defining Access: How Test-Optional Works* (report, National Association for College Admission Counseling, Arlington, VA, April 2018).
44. Troublingly, Geiser observes that the proportion of variation in SAT scores explained by family income, parental education, and race/ethnicity has also increased over the years, pointing to increasing inequality based on demographic traits within the UC system. Geiser, "Race and SAT Scores," 20.
45. While one recent study found that the SAT had a more equitable status as a predictor of achievement for both low- and high-income students, findings are somewhat controversial due to the researchers' status as paid consultants

for the College Board, which runs the SAT. See Scott Jaschik, "Renewed Debate on SAT and Wealth," *Inside Higher Ed*, September 14, 2012, https://www.insidehighered.com/news/2012/09/14/new-research-finds-sat-equally-predictive-those-high-and-low-socioeconomic-status. Geiser, "Race and SAT Scores," 20 (emphasis added).

46. Geiser, "Race and SAT Scores," 20.
47. Ibid.
48. Guinier, *The Tyranny of the Meritocracy*.
49. Natasha K. Warikoo, "Inherent Flaws," *Inside Higher Ed*, May 15, 2017, https://www.insidehighered.com/admissions/views/2017/05/15/essay-reflecting-diversity-and-admissions-process. See also W. Carson Byrd, *Poison in the Ivy: Race Relations and the Reproduction of Inequality on Elite College Campuses* (New Brunswick, NJ: Rutgers University Press, 2017).
50. Sean F. Reardon, "School District Socioeconomic Status, Race, and Academic Achievement," April 2016, https://cepa.stanford.edu/sites/default/files/reardon%20district%20ses%20and%20achievement%20discussion%20draft%20april2016.pdf.

CHAPTER 6

1. Yanan Wang, "Where Justice Scalia Got the Idea that African-Americans Might Be Better Off at 'Slower-Track' Universities," *Washington Post*, December 10, 2015, https://www.washingtonpost.com/news/morning-mix/wp/2015/12/10/where-justice-scalias-got-the-idea-that-african-americans-might-be-better-off-at-slower-track-universities/?utm_term=.8714fb2d9067.
2. Ruth Hamill, Timothy DeCamp Wilson, and Richard E. Nisbett, "Insensitivity to Sample Bias: Generalizing from Atypical Cases," *Journal of Personality and Social Psychology* 39, no. 4 (1980): 378–589; "Group Attribution Error," *Wikipedia*, https://en.wikipedia.org/wiki/Group_attribution_errorhttps://en.wikipedia.org/wiki/Group_attribution_error.
3. Richard Sander and Stuart Taylor Jr., *Mismatch: How Affirmative Action Hurts Students It's Intended to Help, and Why Universities Won't Admit It* (New York: Basic Books, 2012).
4. Claude M. Steele, *Whistling Vivaldi: How Stereotypes Affect Us and What We Can Do*, Issues of Our Time Series (New York: W. W. Norton, 2010).
5. Kevin L. Nadal, Yinglee Wong, Katie E. Griffin, Kristin Davidoff, and Julie Sriken, "The Adverse Impact of Racial Microaggressions on College Students' Self-Esteem," *Journal of College Student Development* 55, no. 5 (2014): 461–74, doi:10.1351/csd.2014.0051; William A. Smith, Man Hung, and Jeremy D. Franklin, "Racial Battle Fatigue and the MisEducation of Black Men: Racial Microaggressions, Societal Problems, and Environmental Stress," *Journal of Negro Education* 80, no. 1 (2011): 63–82; Claude M. Steele and Joshua Aronson, "Stereotype Threat and the Intellectual Test Performance of African

Americans," *Journal of Personality and Social Psychology* 69, no. 5 (1995): 797–811, doi:10.1037/0022-3514.69.5.797.

6. Daniel Solorzano, Miguel Ceja, and Tara Yosso, "Critical Race Theory, Racial Microaggressions, and Campus Racial Climate: The Experience of African American College Students," *Journal of Negro Education* 69, no. 1/2 (2000): 60–73; Tara Yosso, *Critical Race Counterstories Along the Chicana/Chicano Educational Pipeline*, Teaching/Learning Social Justice Series (New York: Routledge, 2005). For a synthesis of this research in STEM, see Maria Ong, Carol Wright, Lorelle Espinosa, and Gary Orfield, "Inside the Double Bind: A Synthesis of Empirical Research on Undergraduate and Graduate Women of Color in Science, Technology, Engineering, and Mathematics," *Harvard Educational Review* 81, no. 2 (2011): 172–209.
7. "Average Student Has Better Chance (77%) of Graduating at Selective Universities Compared to Open Access Schools (51%), Georgetown University Analysis Finds" (press release, Center on Education and the Workforce, McCourt School of Public Policy, Georgetown University, Washington, DC, June 21, 2016), https://cew.georgetown.edu/wp-content/uploads/MismatchFisherUT_pressrelease_6-21-16.pdf.
8. Ibid.
9. Philip U. Treisman, "A Study of the Mathematics Performance of Black Students at the University of California, Berkley" (PhD diss., University of California, Berkeley, 1985); Uri Treisman, "Studying Students Studying Calculus: A Look at the Lives of Minority Mathematics Students in College," *College Mathematics Journal* 23, no. 5 (1992): 362–72.
10. Jason Koebler, "Experts: 'Weed Out' Classes Are Killing STEM Achievement," *U.S. News & World Report*, April 19, 2012, https://www.usnews.com/news/blogs/stem-education/2012/04/19/experts-weed-out-classes-are-killing-stem-achievement.
11. Kenneth D. Gibbs Jr. et al., "Biomedical Science Ph.D. Career Interest Patterns by Race/Ethnicity and Gender," PLOS ONE 9, no. 12 (2014): e114736, doi:10.1371/journal.pone.0114736.12.
12. See, for example, Sander and Taylor, *Mismatch*, 9 ("Because this is mostly an empirical book, our facts are more important than our policy recommendations"), 46 ("Empirical research—that is, *the facts*—had led the two scholars to conclusions . . . "), xiv ("I worked with other scholars and foundations to find and make available databases and funding mechanisms that fostered neutral, careful empirical research on the operation and effects of racial preferences in higher education."), 11 ("The undeniable and extremely disturbing accumulation of evidence of mismatch, primarily through the steadily growing flow of research that this book describes").
13. Ibid., 19.
14. Ibid., 20.

15. Ibid., 44.
16. This percentage ends up being slightly lower than the percentage for Whites due to the differences in absolute numbers for each subcategory. There are more White students than Black students enrolled at the University of Michigan.
17. "Cal State LA Ranked Number One in the Nation for Upward Mobility" (press release, Office of Communications and Public Affairs, California State University, Los Angeles), http://www.calstatela.edu/univ/ppa/publicat/cal-state-la-ranked-number-one-nation-upward-mobility.
18. Steele, *Whistling Vivaldi*. For more on how standardized tests may miss traits that reflect student potential for success, see William E. Sedlacek, *Beyond the Big Test: Noncognitive Assessment in Higher Education* (San Francisco: Jossey-Bass, 2004).
19. For commentary on critiques of research on grit, see Anya Kamenetz, "MacArthur 'Genius' Angela Duckworth Responds to a New Critique of Grit," How Learning Happens Series, NPR, May 25, 2016, http://www.npr.org/sections/ed/2016/05/25/479172868/angela-duckworth-responds-to-a-new-critique-of-grit; Daniel Engber, "Is 'Grit' Really the Key to Success?" *Slate*, May 8, 2016, http://www.slate.com/articles/health_and_science/cover_story/2016/05/angela_duckworth_says_grit_is_the_key_to_success_in_work_and_life_is_this.html.
20. Saul Geiser, "The Growing Correlation Between Race and SAT Scores: New Findings from California" (Research and Occasional Paper Series No. 10.15, Center for Studies in Higher Education, University of California, Berkeley, October 2015), http://www.cshe.berkeley.edu/publications/growing-correlation-between-race-and-sat-scores-new-findings-california-saul-geiser.
21. Sedlacek, *Beyond the Big Test*.
22. For their critique of the Texas system, see Sander and Taylor, *Mismatch*, 280, 288.
23. *Grutter v. Bollinger* (02-241), 539 US 306 (2003) (Justice Thomas dissenting opinion), https://www.law.cornell.edu/supct/html/02-241.ZX1.html.
24. Richard Sander, "A Systemic Analysis of Affirmative Action in American Law Schools," *Stanford Law Review* 57, no. 2 (2004): 367–483.
25. Daniel E. Ho, "Why Affirmative Action Does Not Cause Black Students to Fail the Bar (Scholarship Comment on *A Systemic Analysis of Affirmative Action in American Law Schools*, by Richard H. Sander)," *Yale Law Journal* 114, no. 8 (2005): 1997.
26. David L. Chambers, Timothy T. Clydesdale, William C. Kidder, and Richard O. Lempert, "The Real Impact of Eliminating Affirmative Action in American Law Schools: An Empirical Critique of Richard Sander's Study," *Stanford Law Review* 57 (2005): 1856–98. For even more recent confirmation that eliminating race-conscious admissions in law schools would have no effect on bar passage rates (contrary to the mismatch camp's claims) while having a seriously negative impact on minority enrollments, see Alice Xiang and Donald B. Rubin, "Assessing the Potential Impact of a Nationwide Class-Based Affirmative Action System," *Statistical Science* 30, no. 3 (2015): 297–327, doi:10.1214/15-STS514.

27. Richard H. Sander, "Listening to the Debate on Reforming Law School Admissions Preferences," *Denver University Law Review* 88, no. 4 (2011): 943, http://www.law.du.edu/documents/denver-university-law-review/v88-4/SanderResponse_Final_11311%20(2).pdf.
28. Richard O. Lempert, "University of Michigan Bar Passage 2004–2006: A Failure to Replicate Professor Sander's Results, with Implications for Affirmative Action" (Law & Economics Working Papers 51, University of Michigan Law School, Ann Arbor, 2012), http://repository.law.umich.edu/cgi/viewcontent.cgi?article=1161&context=law_econ_current.
29. For additional summary and critique of Sander's work, as well as commentary on a number of key studies informing the mismatch debate, see Brief for Richard Lempert as Amicus Curiae, *Fisher v. The University of Texas at Austin* (14-981), 579 US Supreme Court (filed November 2015), http://www.scotusblog.com/wp-content/uploads/2015/11/Lempert-Amicus-in-Fisher-v.-U.-Texas-No.-14-981-Filed-Copy.pdf. For good, accessible summaries, see Emily Bazelon, "Sanding Down Sander: The Debunker of Affirmative Action Gets Debunked," *Slate*, April 29, 2005, http://www.slate.com/articles/news_and_politics/jurisprudence/2005/04/sanding_down_sander.html; Richard O. Lempert, "The Supreme Court Has Upheld Affirmative Action, So Let's Dump Mismatch Theory," *New York Times*, June 23, 2016, https://www.nytimes.com/2016/06/24/opinion/the-supreme-court-has-upheld-affirmative-action-so-lets-dump-mismatch-theory.html?_r=0; William Kidder, "A High Target for 'Mimatch': Bogus Arguments About Affirmative Action (review of *Mismatch: How Affirmative Action Hurts Students It's Intended to Help, and Why Universities Won't Admit It*, by Richard Sander and Stuart Taylor Jr.)," *Los Angeles Review of Books*, February 7, 2013, https://lareviewofbooks.org/article/a-high-target-for-mismatch-bogus-arguments-about-affirmative-action/#!.
30. "Average Student Has Better Chance."
31. Ebony O. McGee and Danny B. Martin, "'You Would Not Believe What I Have to Go Through to Prove My Intellectual Value!': Stereotype Management Among Academically Successful Black Mathematics and Engineering Students," *American Education Research Journal* 48, no. 6 (2011): 1347–89; Angela C. Johnson, "Unintended Consequences: How Science Professors Discourage Women of Color," *Science Education* 91, no. 5 (2007): 805–21; Carolyn Justin-Johnson, "Good Fit or Chilly Climate: An Exploration of the Persistence Experiences of African-American Women Graduates of Predominantly White College Science Programs" (PhD diss., University of New Orleans, 2004).
32. Estela M. Bensimon, "The Underestimated Significance of Practitioner Knowledge in the Scholarship of Student Success," *Review of Higher Education* 30, no. 4 (2007): 441–69.
33. William C. Kidder, "Negative Action versus Affirmative Action: Asian Pacific Americans Are Still Caught in the Crossfire," *Michigan Journal of Race and Law* 11 (2005): 613, http://media.asian-nation.org/Kidder-Negative-Action.pdf.

34. Camille L. Ryan and Kurt Bauman, "Educational Attainment in the United States: 2015: Population Characteristics: Current Population Reports" (US Census Bureau, Washington, DC, March 2016), https://www.census.gov/content/dam/Census/library/publications/2016/demo/p20-578.pdf.
35. "Average Student Has Better Chance," 2–3.
36. Sander and Taylor make some not completely terrible suggestions, like preserving race-conscious admissions while giving low-income students a bigger boost, which is something I could get behind. Sander and Taylor, *Mismatch*, 285.
37. Ibid., 279.

CHAPTER 7

1. Hollyn M. Johnson and Colleen M. Seifert, "Sources of the Continued Influence Effect: When Misinformation in Memory Affects Later Inferences," *Journal of Experimental Psychology: Learning, Memory, and Cognition* 20, no. 6 (1994): 1420–36, https://www.researchgate.net/profile/Colleen_Seifert/publication/232501255. For additional insight on why we're oblivious to our blind spots, see Elizabeth Kolbert, "Why Facts Don't Change Our Minds," *The New Yorker*, February 27, 2017, http://www.newyorker.com/magazine/2017/02/27/why-facts-dont-change-our-minds for a summary of compelling studies.
2. Johnson and Seifert, "Sources of the Continued Influence Effect," 1420
3. Sean F. Reardon, Rachel Baker, Matt Kasman, Daniel Klasik, and Joseph B. Townsend, *Can Socioeconomic Status Substitute for Race in Affirmative Action College Admissions Policies? Evidence from a Simulation Model* (Princeton, NJ: Educational Testing Service, 2015), https://www.ets.org/Media/Research/pdf/reardon_white_paper.pdf.
4. "UC San Diego Student Research and Information," http://studentresearch.ucsd.edu/_files/stats-data/enroll/ugethnic.pdf. Still, the dismal reality of UCSD being only 2 percent African American is an improvement—150 percent growth!—over the 1 percent in 2006.
5. A reason why people are too quick to see campuses as highly diverse is that much of the growth in "minority" students or students of color at selective institutions, especially, has come through the higher enrollments of Asian American students, particularly East and South Asian American students, rather than from other underrepresented minority groups. It's not that Asian American growth isn't beneficial for campuses, but it can mask inequities when it allows institutions to throw out numbers such as "we're 40 percent minority" or "well over half of our students are students of color," when really 75 percent of those students of color are Asian American.
6. "UC San Diego Student Research and Information"; "UC Irvine Student Characteristics (Fall 2016)," http://www.oir.uci.edu/files/campus/uci-college-portrait.pdf?R=26562; "UC Berkeley Fall Enrollment Data (Fall 2016)," http://opa.berkeley.edu/uc-berkeley-fall-enrollment-data.

7. "University of Texas, Austin: Facts and Figures," https://www.utexas.edu/about/facts-and-figures.
8. "Enrollment in Texas Public Schools, 2016–2017," 18, http://tea.texas.gov/acctres/enroll_2016-17.pdf.
9. The research on the benefits of diversity establishes how Asian Americans benefit from engaging in a racially diverse student body. See Julie J. Park, *Asian Americans and the Benefits of Campus Diversity: What the Research Says* (Los Angeles: National Commission on Asian American and Pacific Islander Research in Education, 2012), http://care.gseis.ucla.edu/wp-content/uploads/2015/08/CARE-asian_am_diversity_D4.pdf.
10. Soo-yong Byun and Hyunjoon Park, "The Academic Success of East Asian American Youth: The Role of Shadow Education," *Sociology of Education* 85, no. 1 (2012): 54–55, doi:10.1177/0038040711417009; Julie J. Park and Ann H. Becks, "Who Benefits from SAT Prep? An Examination of High School Context and Race/Ethnicity," *Review of Higher Education* 39, no. 1 (2015): 14, doi:10.1353/rhe.2015.0038; Ben Domingue and Derek C. Briggs, "Using Linear Regression and Propensity Score Matching to Estimate the Effect of Coaching on the SAT," *Multiple Linear Regression Viewpoints* 35, no. 1 (2009): 12–29.
11. Nitin Nohria, "We've Gotten Better at Diversity: Now the Challenge Is Inclusion," *Washington Post*, May 19, 2017, https://www.washingtonpost.com/post everything/wp/2017/05/19/weve-gotten-better-at-diversity-now-the-challenge-is-inclusion/?tid=ss_fb&utm_term=.f0cca540fca6.
12. In a detailed case study, administrators at the University of Michigan spoke candidly about how the university shifted from a highly intentional culture committed to championing diversity to one where there was increased silence around race in light of Proposal 2, the ban on race-conscious admissions that followed the university's victory to preserve affirmative action in *Grutter v. Bollinger*. More recently, Michigan has sought to regain ground in this area, but past experience shows that they cannot rest on their laurels. See Liliana M. Garces and Courtney D. Cogburn, "Beyond Declines in Student Body Diversity: How Campus-Level Administrators Understand a Prohibition on Race-Conscious Postsecondary Admissions Policies," *American Educational Research Journal* 52, no. 5 (2015): 828–60.
13. Compare it to the days when Black students were literally excluded from the institution—almost anything is progress if that's your starting point. I'm being partly facetious, but at the same time, it's chilling to remember that people had to argue court cases to achieve the integration that we take for granted today.
14. These concepts are also elaborated on poignantly in Sara Ahmed, *On Being Included: Racism and Diversity in Institutional Life* (Durham, NC: Duke University Press, 2012); and in Natasha K. Warikoo, *The Diversity Bargain and Other Dilemmas of Race, Admissions, and Meritocracy at Elite Universities* (Chicago: University of Chicago Press, 2016). These ideas are also further highlighted in Uma Jayakumar,

Liliana Garces, and Julie J. Park, "Reclaiming Diversity: Advancing the Next Generation of Diversity Research Toward Racial Equity," in the *Higher Education: Handbook of Theory and Research Volume* 33, ed. Michael B. Paulsen (New York: Springer, 2018), 11-80.

15. While diversity certainly falls short without inclusion—really, without a commitment to tackling injustice and systemic exclusion of disenfranchised populations—commitments to inclusion, equity, and justice can also ring hollow without the presence of diversity.
16. When I interviewed members of historically White sororities, they were quick to highlight their diversity—different majors!
17. Maria C. Ledesma, "Complicating the Binary: Toward a Discussion of Campus Climate Health," *Journal Committed to Social Change on Race and Ethnicity* 1 (2016): 6–35, https://www.ncore.ou.edu/media/filer_public/31/10/31105c23-370a-4c07-a666-fb53c286c6b7/maria_c_ledesma_jcscore__spring_2016_.pdf.

Acknowledgments

AS ALWAYS, THERE ARE so many people to thank. I can't name everyone by name, so to everyone who has been a conversation partner with me on race over the years—thank you, thank you. I'm not quite sure how I got the idea to bring in research on cognitive biases to understand how people misunderstand race, but I'm pretty sure that hanging out with "CogSci Mom" Ji Son Kitani over the years had something to do with it, consciously or subconsciously.

This book came about due to a spontaneous conversation with Douglas Clayton at a conference. Thank you, Doug, for your strong support and enthusiastic encouragement from Day 1. Thank you also, Jayne Fargnoli, Sumita Mukherji, and the staff at Harvard Education Press, for ushering the book to print. Jordan Beltran Gonzalez was a wonderful copy editor who helped wrap up the project. Thank you, my dear colleagues and friends at the University of Maryland, College Park, especially Kimberly Griffin, Michelle Espino, and Candace Moore, for all that you do. Many thanks to my students, past and present, for being a continual source of inspiration.

My family is always an unconditional source of love, especially my husband, Daniel, who makes me laugh every day. You make life so good.

I am thankful for the gifts of faith and community. I count myself among those who believe that racism is a permanent and endemic component of American life. Still, I look to the promise that one day, all things will be made new.

Finally, some people say that writing a book is like giving birth. In this case, I was literally pregnant with our son through the development of this project. Thank you, little guy, for waiting in there long enough for me to wrap up writing and also for napping (usually) through the edits. I love you more than I can ever say.

About the Author

JULIE J. PARK, an associate professor of education at the University of Maryland, College Park, studies race, religion, and social class in higher education, including the diverse experiences of Asian American students. Her first book, *When Diversity Drops: Race, Religion, and Affirmative Action in Higher Education* (Rutgers University Press, 2013), addresses how bans on race-conscious admissions affect the everyday lives of students. Her work has also appeared in outlets like the *Washington Post*, *Huffington Post*, and *Chronicle of Higher Education*. She earned her PhD in education from UCLA and BA from Vanderbilt University. Raised in the Midwest, she now calls the Washington, DC, metro region home.

Index